CUTTING ACROSS TIME

CUTTING ACROSS TIME

Logging, Rafting and Milling the Forests of Lake Superior

Mary T. Bell

Nodin Press

Cover Design: Ira Newman

Illustrations: Dale Mann

Watercolors: Lee Weiss

Editors: Judith Brunswick and Lalinda Egerstrom

Layout Design & Production: Rochelle Barnhart
Layout done using Quark XPress 4.0
Body text set in Minion and sidebars in Poppl-Laudatio

Previously published for The Schroeder Area Historical Society, Schroeder, Minnesota

ISBN # 0-931714-84-2

Library of Congress Catalogue Card: #98-061335

Nodin Press, a division of Micawber's, Inc.
525 North Third Street
Minneapolis, MN 55401

Printed by Park Press, Waite Park, MN

Cutting Across Time
is dedicated to those who
make it important to keep history alive
and to those who enjoy looking backward
as much as they enjoy looking forward.

Acknowledgments

In 1991, Betty King, John Schroeder's granddaughter gave the lead donation to build a classroom/office building at Eagle Bluff, an environmental learning center in Lanesboro, Minnesota, and to name it "The John Schroeder Renewable Resources Building." She felt her family's wealth began with her grandfather's success and wanted to give something back. Betty's donation proved critical to Eagle Bluff becoming the first residential environmental learning center in southern Minnesota. In 1991, the Forest Resource Center in Lanesboro, Minnesota, (now renamed Eagle Bluff) compiled A History of John Schroeder and The John Schroeder Lumber Company of Milwaukee, Wisconsin. It was written to answer questions about who John Schroeder was, where he logged and his company.

Minnesota Governor Elmer L. Andersen came across a copy of the first Schroeder book and, after a subsequent series of letters and meetings, we agreed this story was worth retelling. For me, putting this book together was a puzzle. Pieces were locked away in books, libraries, museums and individual recollections. When I found an answer, invariably more questions were uncovered. Information recovery was handicapped by the fact that few Schroeder family and business records or photos survived. Fred Schroeder, Betty's brother, was extremely helpful in providing clues to reconstruct this history.

Angus White, compiler of the first Schroeder book, deserves credit for recording important information. I'm grateful to Ray Howe of Lone Oak Press for his support and encouragement at every step of pulling this book together. Laurie Geisler deserves recognition for her layout development assistance. My good friend Jack Pichotta helped develop the friendly voice. Thanks to Sally Zank for finding so many interesting anecdotes. Sandra Bennett, President of The Schroeder Area Historical Society graciously responded above and beyond the call of duty. Jan Young from the Superior Lumber Company was a treat to work with in uncovering valuable pieces and parts. And I am grateful to my husband, Joe Deden, a forester, who read each draft with interest and suggestions.

Personal interviews were the most fun and informative. Throughout these pages you'll meet some great people. Bob Silver knows the Cross River and its history. Pat Labadie, Director of the Army Corps of Engineers, Lake Superior Visitor's Center in Duluth, Minnesota knows Lake Superior and its vessels. Fred Mackie worked summers as a youth on a tug hauling pulpwood log rafts to Ashland. John Walters worked 40 years in forestry, 27 of which were in the pulpwood industry. Ed Erickson, a Bayfield, Wisconsin, native spent his life exploring the Apostle Islands. These people provided substance and character to this book and deserve credit and heartfelt appreciation.

—*Mary Bell*

Contents

Foreword

In some ways, this book fills out a family story about my grand-uncle, Jim Harvinson. Around the turn of the 19th Century logging in the pinery of the North Woods was second only to farming as a means of making a living in Minnesota. Like many men in my native state Harvinson worked at both. He was, by report, a big man—six-foot three or more and well over 200 pounds, and a bachelor. He worked his Minnesota farm in the summer. Winter, with his axes in a sling, Jim always headed north to work in the lumber camps until spring. I was also told he was a famous wood chopper, which implies many things the reader of this work will be able to appreciate as Mary Bell's descriptions of life in the logging camps unfold.

This book is also a historical fulfillment. It reports on an aspect of the economic development and to some extent the exploitation of the resources of the upper midwest (Minnesota, Wisconsin and Michigan) for more than 75 years, from 1850 to 1927. It tells of the initiatives of one businessman, John Schroeder, and the men—the lumberjacks, horse drivers, tug men, cooks, bookkeepers—who operated his enterprises. Common men doing the customary work of their times, like men of any other time, building their lives, and a country, from the things at hand.

—*Senator Eugene McCarthy*

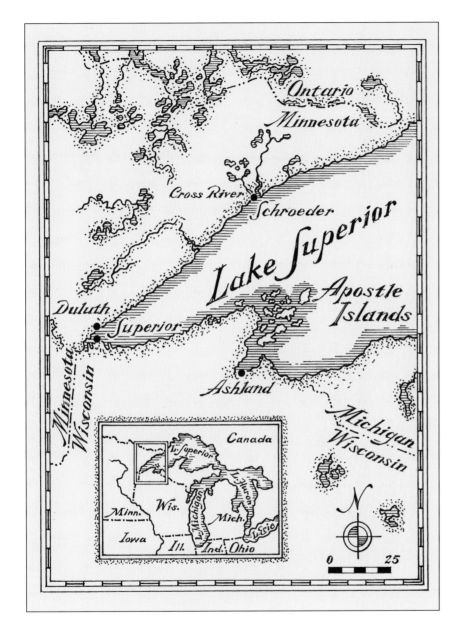

Introduction

Telling how John Schroeder logged pine, other softwoods and hardwoods in northeastern Minnesota and the Apostle Islands lends color and vitality to the past. Towering white pine were cut, rafted and pulled by tugs across Lake Superior to Schroeder's lumber mill in Ashland, Wisconsin. In addition, pine, hardwood and pulpwood from the Apostle Islands—Oak, Michigan, Outer and Stockton—buoyed Ashland's economy for more than 30 years.

At the Cross River in northeastern Minnesota, pines were cut and stacked through the winters of 1901 through 1905. In order for the Schroeder Company to get logs from the back country, changes were made to the Cross River. Seven dams were constructed to hold back water from the spring ice melt. This water transported the logs out of the woods. Wooden chutes and sluiceways were constructed through gorges and down the waterfalls to minimize log jams during the river drive. The top of the Cross River waterfall was dynamited and sheared flat to reroute the flow of water. Each spring, when the water was high enough, the river floated the logs down to Lake Superior where they were caught in a holding boom, then rafted to the Schroeder's Ashland mill. Schroeder cut two hundred million feet of white pine from Lake and Cook counties in northern Minnesota. When this area was cleared, the company focused on the Apostle Islands.

John Schroeder was a successful parent, church leader and business person. Historical records of his community, church and family attest to that fact. As time passes, the depth of written history is often made more intense and personal due to the work of those who search for stories and facts found in personal accounts, letters, diaries and newspapers. The intent of this book is to use the story of John Schroeder to look at the places and events involved in logging around Lake Superior at the turn of the 20th century.

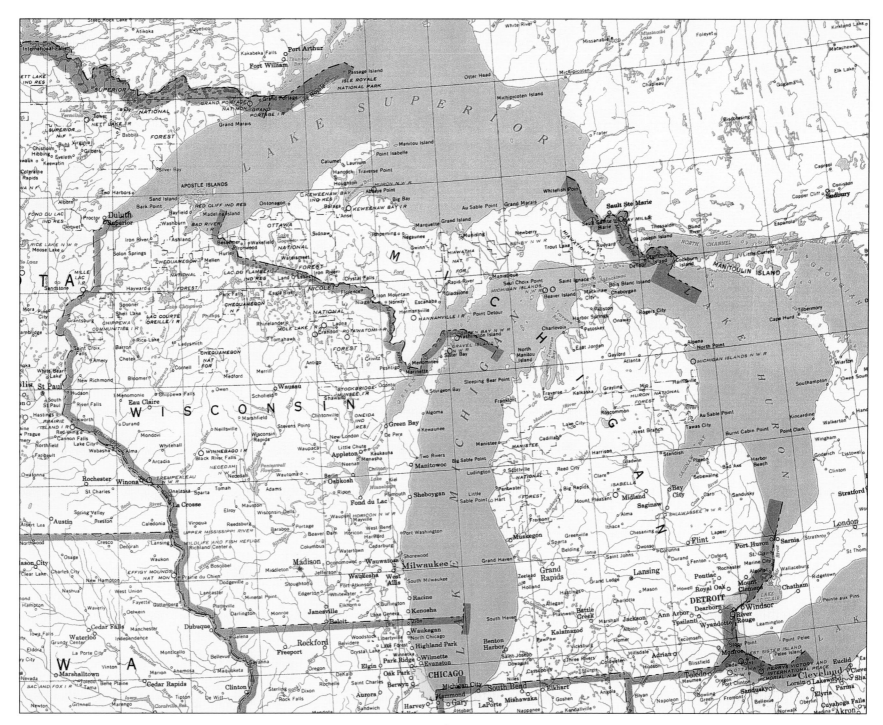

CHAPTER ONE

The Schroeder Enterprise

John and Margaretha Schroeder

From Hanover, Germany to Milwaukee, Wisconsin

John Schroeder was born in Hanover, Germany, on December 8, 1827, and christened Christian Ferdinand Schroeder. In 1837, John and his parents, Franz Wilhelm Schroeder and Clara Elizabeth (Koring) Schroeder, immigrated to the United States and settled in St. Louis, Missouri. Franz did carpentry work and Clara washed clothes in a hotel. Young John attended a Lutheran parochial school until his father died. After that he worked as a wagon driver to help support his mother.

Like his parents, John did not hesitate to accept whatever work was available. In 1846, he left home, moved to Milwaukee, Wisconsin, and worked as a grocery store clerk. Within months he had saved enough money to purchase a wagon and a team of horses and formed a partnership with a newfound friend, Byron Abert. Together they moved immigrants and their belongings from Milwaukee into other parts of the upper Midwest. John and Byron also used their teams to do road and building site grade work and were well known for good work at a fair price.

One fall John took a number of families into the Nebraska Territory. Later he heard that these settlers had suffered through a bad winter. So he brought them additional food and supplies when he returned in the spring with another group of settlers. That act and others like it contributed to John's growing reputation as a decent and honest businessman.

John also provided carrier service for a number of timber companies. His habit of taking good care of his horses led to his being in a barn late one night. He heard several men plotting to steal $50 in gold that he was delivering to a lumber camp as payroll for a crew of Peshtigo, Wisconsin, lumberjacks. Knowing their plans, John was able to prevent the theft by getting up in the middle of the night, hitching up the horses and escaping.

Courtesy Marilyn Kiekhefer Fifield, Great granddaughter

John Schroeder, 1827–1908.

Courtesy Marilyn Kiekhefer Fifield, Great granddaughter

Margaretha Schroeder, 1841–1913.

Courtesy The Milwaukee Journal Home Section, October 8, 1967

The Schroeder Mansion.

As Milwaukee grew, so did the demand for land grading. Hills had to be leveled and swamps and marshes filled. Due in large part to that demand, John Schroeder and Byron Abert became successful businessmen with all the work they could handle.

John Schroeder and Margaretha Luehring marry

In August 1846, Johann Heinrich Luehring and Anna Wintherst Luehring immigrated to Milwaukee from Hanover, Germany, with their two daughters, five-year-old Margaretha and three-year-old Sophie.

Henry and Anna ran a blacksmith shop, a grocery store and a tavern on Greenfield Avenue in addition to maintaining a farm west of Milwaukee on Loomis Road. Henry was an entrepreneur who enjoyed both his businesses and his role. At the end of his work day he'd dress in a white linen suit and on horseback inspect his workers and their daily accomplishments. Henry regularly returned to Germany to purchase goods ranging from farm implements to lace for resale in one of his businesses.

On March 2, 1859, at age 32, John Schroeder wedded 19-year-old Margaretha Luehring. Their marriage resulted in 12 children and 27 grandchildren. In 1880 the Schroeders purchased a home adequate for their growing family.

The Schroeder home at 504 West Galena Street

By 1890, John's business had successfully diversified into the lumber industry. A carpenter's son, John loved wood and had access to unlimited supply—all the resources he needed to remodel his home. Time, and the influence of architect Eugene R. Leibert, transformed the Schroeder home into the Schroeder Mansion. What started as an $8,000 addition became one of the finest homes in Milwaukee's affluent Uihlein Hill neighborhood.

Bold carved heads were placed on beam ends that supported the eaves and adorned the massive front doors. The imposing brown brick exterior featured numerous balconies and decks fortified by Teutonic forms, medieval roof braces, elaborate timber work, heavy wrought iron railings, tie rods and basement window grills. All of the second-floor balconies were framed in six-inch carved wooden beams. An iron sundial decorated the third-floor octagonal tower.

The mansion was indeed elaborate

The living room featured a hand-carved curly birch mantel and six sliding doors of perfectly matched grain. The center of the floor was constructed to bring their exquisite rugs flush to the adjoining parquet floors. Elegantly painted cherubs adorned each of three oval ceiling panels. Onyx slabs lined the fireplace. The window sills were green marble. Bronze cherubs decorated two gilt rococo chandeliers. The south-facing windows were all stained glass.

The connecting dining room had a glazed ornamental tile mantelpiece with a 5½ foot plaster frieze of 15 carved cherubs. Six adages, all in German, were carved into the oak heads. One said, "A joke without salt is farmer's lard." The kitchen walls were covered, floor to ceiling, with hundreds of imported Delft tiles, and the conservatory featured glazed white-tiled walls.

The world-famous Schlitz Park was only a few blocks from the Schroeder mansion. On week nights and weekends, the Schroeders' wealthy neighbors enjoyed concerts and operas, played cards, bowled, held meetings and enjoyed large family picnics. The Schroeder family surely participated in the social events conducted at Schlitz Park, their status apparent in the opulence of the Schroeder Mansion.

St John's Evangelical Lutheran Church

Church was very important to John and Margaretha Schroeder. In 1848, at the age of 21, John Schroeder became a founding member of

Courtesy Pastor Keith Hasting, St. John's Evangelical Lutheran Church
This magnificent altar was a gift from the Schroeder family.

Courtesy Pastor Keith Hasting, St. John's Evangelical Lutheran Church
The Rev. Johannes P. Bading, the Schroeders' pastor and friend.

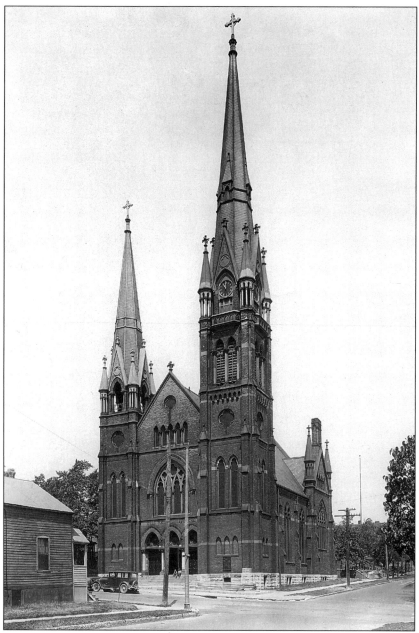

Courtesy Pastor Keith Hasting, St. John's Evangelical Lutheran Church

St. John's Evangelical Church, a Gothic structure built of Cream City brick and limestone, was designed by Architect Scnetzky. Its 200-foot steeple has three bells, each weighing over two tons.

St. John's Church and was committed to both the development of a proper edifice and to increasing its membership. In 1856, John became church president and remained a life-long council member. From then until 1890, when the new church was dedicated, John and Margaretha's home often served as a meeting place.

John Schroeder put a great deal of energy and money into building St. John's Church. In 1868, the church had 28 members, and by 1890 the membership had increased to more than 500. The new church cost $65,000 to build and seated 1,200 people.

St. John's Church was elemental to family life for its members. It helped solve family disputes, mitigated legal issues and provided a spiritual home to many of Milwaukee's most prominent citizens. Pastor Johannes P. Bading conducted all services in German from 1868 through 1908.

John Schroeder companies

In 1866, John at age 39 made a decisive move to form a partnership with a man already established in the lumber business, Martin Seyfried. The Schroeder & Seyfried Lumber Company at 541 River Street in Milwaukee lasted until 1872 when Seyfried retired. John's business continued as John Schroeder & Company.

The John Schroeder & Company business grew to include a west side yard in 1873; a northside yard in 1875, and a southside facility to complete the Milwaukee operation in 1880. A hardwood floor manufacturing plant was located at Walnut and Commerce streets. Corporate offices were housed at Park and Virginia Streets, and a sales office was maintained in Chicago, Illinois.

On April 15, 1881, the John Schroeder Lumber Company was incorporated as a joint stock company. John and each of his three sons received a one-quarter interest. John served as president; Henry, vice-president; Fred, secretary, and William, treasurer. Henry succeeded his father as president after John died in 1908 and held that position until his own death in 1919. Fred then ran the company until it was liquidated in 1939.

Schroeder was successful not only because of access to excellent rail and dock facilities, but for its reputation for fair dealing, honest lumber grading, excellent millwork and a vast array of wood products. It grew into one of the largest and most complete retailers of northern, southern and western U.S. lumber.

A focus on quality

The Schroeder Company offered its customers a nearly unlimited choice of perfectly milled wood products. One, a "polished to perfection" hardwood flooring, had a deep, rich shine reflecting perfectly matched wood grains. A double-drying process used steam pressure to open wood pores, then hot kiln air dried the flooring evenly so that it never warped.

With such high standards, competitive prices could be maintained because of Schroeder's vertically integrated business structure. The company owned and operated every step of the lumber business, from logging and transporting its own timber to processing it into finished products. The Schroeder Company purchased a lumber mill in Ashland, Wisconsin, in 1901.

The company averaged 500 employees, counting woods workers, mill employees and lumberyard staff. Milwaukee's four locations employed 75 to 125 people and had average annual sales of 18 million board feet of lumber, lath, shingles, pickets and posts. The Ashland mill's average annual output was 75 million board feet of lumber valued at two million dollars.

Schroeder Company Main Yards.

This 1896 Schroeder ad is from the Milwaukee Lumber Association.

Where is the Cross River?

The Cross River drains an area of 91 square miles in Lake and Cook counties in Minnesota. The main stream source is Bone Lake and flows through Frear, Timber, Elbow, Finger and the Cross River lakes before it actually begins as a stream. Below Cross River Lake, it flows three miles as a fairly rapid stream about 15 feet wide, where it receives three major tributaries: Wilson Lake outlet, Four Mile Creek and Wanless Creek. Below the entrance of Wanless Creek, the Cross River runs about six miles through long ponded stretches separated by short rapids. Many of these pools are 50 feet wide. In the northwest quarter of Section 15, the stream narrows to about 30 feet and flows quickly over a stony bottom to the falls, about a mile below the Four Mile Creek road crossing. Between the upper falls, which are 40 feet high, and Lake Superior, the stream drops over five waterfalls ranging in height from 12 to 90 feet.

A Biological Survey and Fishery Management Plan
for the Streams of the Lake Superior North Shore Watershed

Schroeder's Cross River serves as an example of his operation

Schroeder's forest land holdings included white pine in Lake and Cook counties in northeastern Minnesota. The company logged about 18,000 acres of land near Ontonagon and Bessemer, Michigan. Thousands of acres near Saxon and Oronto Creek in Wisconsin were harvested, as were approximately 150 square miles of pine and mixed timber around Thunder Bay, Ontario, Canada. About 23,000 acres of longleaf pine were cut near the headwaters of the Sarasota River in Florida, and an additional 112,000 acres near Tampa were logged. The company also cut 21,000 acres of pine in Oregon.

How the Cross River got its name

In 1846, Father Frederic Baraga, a Wisconsin missionary, heard an epidemic was taking its toll on Chippewa (Ojibwa) Indians living in Grand Portage, Minnesota. He hired Louis Gaudin, an Indian guide, and in a small canoe they sailed across Lake Superior from La Pointe, Wisconsin, to Grand Portage. During the crossing, the wind changed to a northeasterly direction and forced them to paddle through a bad storm. They were nearly lost. The boat almost swamped. They could have been smashed by the enormous waves along the rocky shore. Through a stroke of luck, or the will of God, they entered the mouth of a small river and found safety. When on shore, Father Baraga made a small cross from a tree to commemorate their "miraculous salvation" and named the river Cross River. When the storm subsided, they sailed on to Grand Portage.

Thomas Clark, an engineer and surveyor, noted in his October 27, 1854, diary entry that he saw Father Baraga's cross while on a surveying trip from Superior, Wisconsin, to Grand Marais, Minnesota.

The Cross River area became Redmyer

Henry J. Redmyer was one of the first North Shore settlers in the 1880s. The Redmyer family came from reindeer country in northern Norway. Henry recorded a land claim for a parcel on the west bank at the mouth of the Cross River in1886.

The settlement of Redmyer was official on March 23, 1888, when the post office opened. Hedley, Henry's son, was Redmyer's first and only postmaster. Redmyer lost its post office when one opened on December 15, 1891, in Lutsen, ten miles to the north. When the lake was navigable, a boat brought the mail three times a week. In winter, a dog sled or a horse and sleigh brought mail from the town of Two Harbors.

Redmyer became Schroeder

In 1901, William Dolan, superintendent of Schroeder's logging operation, applied for a post office in the village, which was one-half mile west of Schroeder's logging camp. Dolan became the first postmaster. In 1905, the post office moved into a corner of the hotel dining room, and William C. Smith became the postmaster.

The town of Schroeder was organized in 1904. William C. Smith, A. G. Frandenburg, Gilbert Johnson and J. Reynolds served as clerks on the first town board. The first town hall was built in 1923.

Courtesy Patricia Hegg Brown, Great granddaughter
Hedley Redmyer

Courtesy Patricia Hegg Brown, Great granddaughter
Emilie Redmyer

Courtesy Patricia Hegg Brown, Great granddaughter
The Redmyer homestead at Cross River.

The Schroeder hotel and old bridge about 1920.

Robert (Bob) Silver was born in 1913. As a young man, he helped his dad "cruise" timber. He has lived all his life in the Schroeder area. He knows the Cross River and its history.

The Schroeder Tote Road
As written and told by Bob Silver

The year was 1895, Grover Cleveland was our president. It was the year the John Schroeder Lumber Company of Milwaukee commenced its logging operation at Cross River.

I suppose it was reports from diaries of those who made the first government survey of the North Shore in 1859 (the president was James Buchanan then) that started the rumors. Comments such as, 'You should see the beautiful white pine on the Cross River watershed, the trees are thick and tall with little or no undergrowth. It would make you think of a park.' Alert timber cruisers kept mental notes of conversations such as this. My guess is Schroeder Company cruisers became aware of untouched stands of white pine in just such a way. When Schroeder's cruisers presented this information to him, I imagine he was very quick to have his men check it out.

A four-man cruising and estimating crew was probably the most practical. The crew would have consisted of two cruisers—one would have been the chief, the third a compass man and the fourth an experienced cook.

In the early 1800s, there was a small Native American settlement at Pork Bay in Lake County. A well-used and well-maintained trail called the Pork Bay Trail ran inland from Lake Superior. Some old timers called it the Hudson Bay Trail because it connected to other trails to Hudson Bay. It was about 12 miles south of the Cross River. An Indian, Jim Gesick, said his people walked this trail in 1820. It ran through the headwaters of the Cross River through stands of white pine. The cruising party probably got off the boat and walked as far as 15 miles from the lake, picked out the nicest spot on the river bank, near spring water, pitched their tent and called it their headquarters. They'd want to be on the river to make notes about how long it held a high flow after a rain.

In 1859, the United States government survey recorded the section lines, corner posts and bearing trees along the Cross River. Section lines marked the perimeter of each square mile. It was the cruiser's responsibility to locate and estimate the quantity and quality of all marketable species in each of the 16 forty-acre parcels that make up a section. With camp set up, the cruiser and his compass man immediately commenced estimating timber section-by-section.

The chief cruiser would have been a man with experience in all phases of logging, including river drives. First he'd walk the section lines East, West, North and South to determine how large a timber area the Cross River watershed encompassed. The head cruiser soon realized there was a large quantity of white pine in the Cross River watershed.

The Cross River itself was the cruiser's next concern. He'd walk up and down the river noting the drawbacks in conducting a log drive and how these obstacles might be overcome. He would have noticed the beaver were unable to make their dams hold on the river. That would have told him the spring runoff was favorable for floating logs. While at Lake Superior he no doubt had long conversations with Henry Redmyer. Redmyer lived at the mouth of the Cross River prior to the cruiser's visit and could have provided lots of information on the river and the lake.

His attention then turned to building a good road 15 to 20 miles long. Where should it be and how much would construction cost for a logging operation of this size? It was essential the tote road be able to accommodate four-horse teams hitched to heavy wagons and sleighs.

When men were real "cruisers"

Cruisers were also called landlookers or surveyors. They used compasses, Indian guides and tree marks to pace out and locate timber. The cruiser determined the type of trees, where they were, and any potentially serious harvesting problems in order to estimate how many million board feet a stand could yield. A single tree could yield 5,000 board feet of lumber. A board foot is a measure of sawed lumber one foot square and one inch thick.

Landlooker in the Upper Peninsula of Michigan

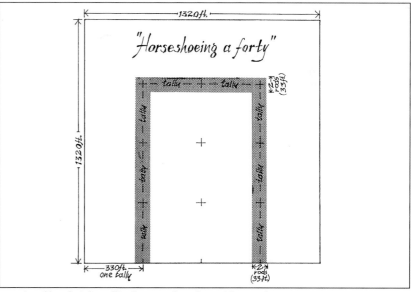

A strip of land eight tallies long and 33 feet wide equals two acres. In cruiser language, this is called "horseshoeing a forty." In every tally, the cruiser made notes on the timber, especially the white pine.

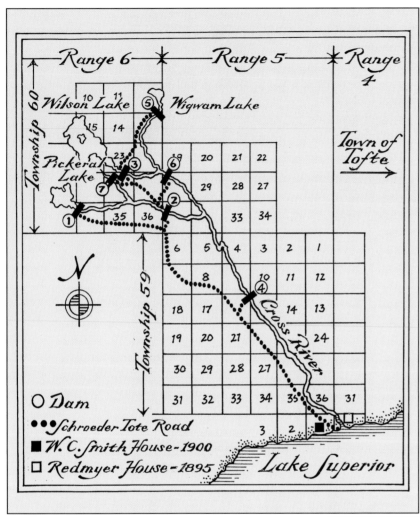

The Schroeder Tote Road.
Bob Silver's mother and father walked this trail to get to their homestead in 1900.

Original drawing: Bob Silver

It was no small task to locate this road in the best possible place at the least cost. One should remember that at that time, John Schroeder did not yet have title to the Cross River timber stumpage. Cruisers came to carefully investigate if a complex logging operation in this remote and rugged area was feasible. That was the question! This cruising party answered this question in about six weeks. Their report must have sounded favorable to John Schroeder because he purchased the timber stumpage, leased property from Henry Redmyer and the Schroeder operation was under way.

The next order of business was to send a skeleton crew of camp builders to construct the cookhouse and bunkhouse. The men lived in tents until the buildings were habitable. It's a good possibility that the logs used in construction came off the Redmyer property. As camp construction continued, a horse barn, root cellar and other buildings were built.

While camp construction was going on, it's likely those first two cruisers would have been back on the job for Schroeder. This time their first duty would be to blaze out the Tote Road. They would have marked the center line of the road. Back in those days, all logging roads were cleared, stumps grubbed and leveled by station workers. A station is a 100-foot portion of any road and to whatever width was determined. …

When the Tote Road was completed to the first logging campsite, the teamsters with their four-horse teams began the never-ending task of hauling logging supplies. It's hard to imagine the vast quantity of materials toted to all the camps and the dam sites: hay, oats and corn for the horses, and flour, sugar, dried fruit, lard, bacon, canned goods, potatoes, large camp cook stoves, utensils and much more. Large quantities of kerosene were essential to each camp. A couple of lanterns burned all night in the bunkhouse *for the lumberjacks who sought out the facilities behind. Several kerosene lamps burned in the cookhouse. The teamsters, bull cook and barn boss had lanterns. All sawyers carried a bottle of kerosene in their back pocket for keeping their cross-cut saws free of pitch. The kerosene had to be hauled in wagons over rough roads without spilling any on the food supplies. In addition, there were the tons of blacksmith supplies, all the logging tools, cant hooks, peaveys, saws, neck yokes and axes that had to be toted to the various logging sites. There was a host of other items, including telephone wire and insulators for the telephone that ran from the shore of Lake Superior to all camps and dams. The Schroeder Tote Road ran to every one of the logging camps and to each of the seven dam sites.*

The Schroeder logging camp at the Cross River.

The Schroeder logging camp

In 1900, Schroeder leased Henry Redmyer's land and buildings at the west side of the mouth of the Cross River for a five-year period. In fall, men started showing up for work. Many were farmers who worked in the woods during the winter to make extra money. Some men logged throughout the winter and worked in the mills the rest of the year. Logging was men's business; few women were to be found.

Trees were cut and ground was leveled. Then construction began on camp buildings. Bottom logs, 40 feet long with 20-inch butts and 9-inch tops were stacked on top of each other, side to side. When the logs reached three high, the window and door frames were set in. More logs were rolled up and put butt-against-end and the seams chinked with moss. Some outside walls were earth-bermed. The roof was covered with tar paper to keep moisture out. Rough sawn lumber was used for flooring.

As many as 100 men slept in each bunkhouse. Bunkhouses were 60 to 80 feet long and 24 to 30 feet wide with windows on each end and a front and back door. Eight-foot sidewalls supported a gently pitched roof. At least one skylight, held open by a notched pole, helped control the temperature and ventilate the odor of wet, pungent wool clothes worn by hard-working men. Rows of double-decked wooden bunks— each bunk about four feet wide, six feet long and eight inches deep— provided sleeping space. These hard, wooden beds were softened with hay, evergreen boughs or straw. Straw was preferred, even though it fell down on the bunk below, because it could easily be removed, burned and replaced. Grain sacks filled with straw served as pillows. Warm, gray, wool blankets and a cast-iron stove, placed in a shallow box filled with sand, provided warmth during North Shore winters. Wires hung from the wood stove chimney provided places to hang wet clothes. Men sat on chairs made from split logs with smoothed tops, called deacon benches. Cedar chips scattered on the floor helped repel lice and ticks. The bull cook supplied wood, mopped floors, hauled water and filled the kerosene lanterns.

The health of a camp was very important

Logging camps prior to the turn of the century were often breeding grounds for disease. But by the time of the Schroeder camps, vaccinations were available. Above all, loggers valued good water. Bob Silver said, "The Cross River continuously flows under the ice. At inland camps they tapped springs and melted snow."

Outhouses and barns were always constructed away from the water supply. They were rough, roofed shacks over open pits, constructed at least 100 feet downwind from the bunkhouses. Lime or dirt was tossed into the pit to help control the odor and decompose the waste. Some-times, at the end of one logging season, outhouses were burned and holes filled. New ones were constructed the next season.

Men washed at sinks at the end of the bunkhouse. At first, wooden barrels were filled with water, but over time they used 55-gallon metal drums with pipes coming directly from the wood stove's firebox to provide hot water. Lye soap, a few clean towels and pails of cold drinking water were supplied by the bull cook.

Weekends were the time to bathe. Bob Silver recalled, "Lumberjacks had a washhouse that contained a large cast-iron box stove. The stove took sticks of wood 40 inches long. The top of the stove was a cast-iron top with three 10-inch lids. The local Finlanders placed stones all around the stove, as high as the top, and when the stones got hot, they threw hot water on them to create a sauna."

Some men shaved. They would cut each other's hair. Sunday was the time to wash clothes. They built a fire outside to heat water and in an iron washtub, they literally "boiled up" their clothes. Once clean, clothes were hung to dry on tree branches or shrubs.

Injuries happened

Broken bones, the most common injury, generally were set by someone from the company. Saloon fights during off hours also took a toll. One can only imagine, when men worked and slept together from November to April, that boredom or individual differences may have led to disagreements, fights and injuries. Physicians were scarce. Loggers were able to buy a type of insurance from hospital agents for $10 a year in case of sickness or injury.

Staying warm and dry

"The temperature during North Shore winters could reach 40 degrees below, but if you dressed right, you could stay warm." Bob Silver suggested, "Put a light wool sweater over wool underwear, then put on heavy wool shirts."

Edward Silver used oxen to haul moose out of the woods.

Keeping warm was a priority for the lumberjack. He wore wool long johns, plaid wool shirts, heavy wool pants and two pair of (hopefully) dry wool socks. Wool was the preferred fabric because it absorbed sweat. Bob Silver recalled, "My dad wore blackish-grey Malone pants. They were the most popular brand. Lumberjacks cut their pant legs off at mid-calf to minimize ice collecting on them. Wide suspenders were always part of the outfit." They wore Mackinaw coats and thick wool "Scotch" caps that stood up high on top of their heads. According to Bob Silver, "This cap was the only safety helmet the lumberjack had." Some wore stocking or visored wool caps with ear flaps. Their leather mittens, called "choppers," had red, white or blue wool liners.

Footwear was extremely important. Heavy leather boots were waterproofed with tallow, beeswax, or bear grease heated in a large can on the wood stove. A stick with a cloth wrapped around one end was dipped into the hot liquid, an adequate amount was put on the boot, then it was hand-rubbed into the leather.

During navigable weather, Lake Superior was the "road" by which all supplies were brought to the base camp. In winter, travel was limited because the ice wasn't safe. In 1898 Alger Smith, the largest North Shore logging operation, brought the Duluth & Northern railroad to Two Harbors, 60 miles southwest of Schroeder. As an example of the quantity of supplies needed, the Alger Smith Logging Company's annual grocery bill was $250,000, which included 365 sacks of beans that weighed 165 pounds each. Their annual tobacco bill was $25,000.

Local farmers sold potatoes and other root crops to the camp cook. "Wild" Bill Premble had a cabin in the woods and bartered moose meat with the camp cook for groceries. Fishermen and hunters provided fresh fish and game. On Sundays, during seasons Lake Superior was free of ice, men fished from the shore and in boats. In winter, they fished through holes cut in the ice. Schroeder camps always had pigs and cattle to provide fresh, accessible meat.

The cookhouse was wider and longer than the bunkhouse. Often a covered passageway connected the doorways. This provided a convenient spot to store barrels of corned beef, boxes of smoked sausage and fish, as well as a protected passageway from bunkhouse to cookhouse.

In winter, the outdoors served as refrigerator and freezer. Root cellars constructed near the cookhouse door were cavelike depressions dug into the side of a hill. They were shored up and roofed over with rafters and soil. The earth-bermed walls protected potatoes, rutabagas, onions, cabbage, turnips and carrots from freezing.

Windows and skylights let light into the cookhouse kitchen. Stove pipes vented smoke from large, two-oven wood stoves. Sinks drained through spouts pushed out through the cookhouse walls. Walls held shelves of tin dishes and utensils. Hooks held iron kettles and skillets. Barrels of flour, dried beans, rice, peas, barley, macaroni, sugar, tapioca, raisins, currants, dried apples, prunes, peaches and apricots were stacked along the walls. Big wooden kegs with spigots were filled with syrup and molasses. Bob Silver said, "Men ate syrup on everything—beans, flapjacks, even rice." Food was served and eaten from tin plates and bowls. Gallon tins held baking soda, baking powder, salt, canned milk and tomatoes.

Cookhouse Rules

#1 come in

#2 sit down

#3 shut up

#4 eat fast

#5 get out

In her re-enactment of a logging camp cook, Terry McLaughlin, Director of Naturalist Training at Wolf Ridge Environmental Learning Center, located only a few miles from Schroeder, provided five rules for lumberjacks coming into her cookhouse.

They ate a lot, and they ate fast

The head cook and his assistants, the cookees, were out of bed before 5 a.m. to prepare breakfast. The wake-up call sounded and, before long, men came into the cookhouse and sat down. They were served a hearty breakfast of flapjacks as big as dinner plates, fried meat, potatoes, eggs, fresh sourdough bread and biscuits, doughnuts, gingerbread, oatmeal, prunes and tea. Dried prunes, considered a lumberjack's tonic, were popular at every meal.

Each man had his own place on the pine board bench. The 40-foot table was covered with oilcloth. The only conversation was to get something passed. Cookees kept busy refilling serving dishes.

After breakfast, the men walked to work with full stomachs. Those working in the woods had their dinner delivered by a chore boy around 11:30 a.m. Large cans containing hot food were brought by a horse-driven sleigh. This was a big meal: Mulligan stew or hot beef sandwiches, mashed potatoes, gravy and fresh bread, followed by warm pie. Those working too far away to get to the sleigh, carried a nosebag. This was an oilcloth backpack containing fresh bread sandwiches piled high with sliced meat. Dessert was generally a ginger cookie one-half- to five-eighths-inch thick and 8 inches in diameter.

After a long day's work, the men returned to camp for supper. Schroeder cooks served a variety of meat: roast beef, tenderloin steak, sweetbreads, liver, short beef ribs, pig's feet, pork sausages, sowbelly, corned beef, pork loin and hamburger. Rice, fresh bread and pots of beans were staples. Often there was pea soup or venison stew with hot biscuits; for dessert, fresh baked raisin, apple, peach, mincemeat or currant pie, corn bread, rice pudding, pound cake or sugar cookies. Bakery goods were the cheapest thing to feed hungry men. The standard beverages were coffee and tea, the latter considered by some to be more refreshing and a better stimulant. After supper, cookies, pies and snacks were always available on a cookhouse table.

Schroeder camp cooks worked at least 15 hours a day for months, with no time off, to feed several hundred hungry men three substantial meals. Schroeder had a reputation for good food, decent living conditions and fair wages. Without good food, men wouldn't stay.

Every job was important

Some jobs paid more and had higher status. For example, cooks and blacksmiths earned more than the men who cut down trees. Wages included board and bunk. An average day was 10 to 12 hours. Men worked six days a week. Each man kept track of his day's work. Payday came once a month. Logging terminology and job responsibilities changed from camp to camp. Generally the job depended on the number of men available. In some camps, swampers branded logs while in others, deckers or chainers did that job.

The daily wage of a foreman in 1889-90 was $2.40; cooks earned $2 and swampers $1.25. In 1895, woods workers' wages dropped to $18 to $26 per month. In 1897, the average annual wage for workers in the industry was $386. At the turn of the century, the Schroeder Company paid its common laborers between $16 and $30 per month; a two-horse teamster earned $30, a four-horse teamster made $35 and a foreman earned $40. Men who brought their own team received separate pay for themselves and their horses. Sometimes a team of horses earned more than its driver.

Blacksmiths were crucial in a successful logging operation. At night, when the horses returned to the barn, the blacksmith replaced horseshoes that pulled off or loosened during the day. The blacksmith shod horses, repaired equipment and made supplies. His shop, near the barn and road, was about 24 feet square. His tools included a forge, hand bellows, anvil, vises and hammers. In one corner was the shoeing floor with various sizes of horseshoes and nails. Chains of various sizes hung from the walls. Blank nuts, to be threaded as needed, came in an assortment of sizes in 100-pound kegs. A forge stood in one corner with a wooden funnel overhead for smoke to escape. Dry aspen and coal provided the welding heat. The blacksmith squeezed the bellows to generate air flow. To weld, two steel bars were heated in the white-hot coals of the forge. Once hot, the ends were placed on an anvil, flattened and fused into one piece with quick, precise blows from the blacksmith's hammer.

The better a saw was filed, the faster and easier it cut. For the filer to do his job right, he needed to have good light and be able to concentrate. His shack was in an open area close to the logging site. He was expert at applying the exact amount of pressure against the saw teeth, at the right angle, with the correct stroke. Saw teeth had varied shapes and patterns. "Cutters" cut through the wood and "rakers" pulled sawdust away. Rakers and cutters alternated on the saw blade.

Horses were prized

Great care was taken to prevent horses from getting too hot or cold. Barn roof vents let steam out when horses came in warm. Horses left standing in the woods were covered with blankets. Barns provided storage space for straw, harness, log chains and other equipment. The barn boss cleaned the barn morning and night. The horses were watered and fed hay, oats and corn.

Horses provided the muscle power to move logs, men and supplies. Percherons, Belgians and Morgans weighing an average of 1600 to 1800 pounds and about eight years old worked best in the northwoods. Schroeder had company horses, some teamsters brought their own and local residents leased their teams.

Two-man cross-cut saws became common about 1870. Their upright round handles at each end were grasped with both hands. Cross-cut saw blades were about 6½ feet long. The blade had two cutting teeth followed by a raker to clear sawdust from the cutter's path. A 1922 Marshall Wells Wholesale Hardware Catalog sold cross-cut saws without handles for $6.80 each and $14.60 with handles.

Clerks, a.k.a. ink slingers or bookkeepers

Clerks were the timekeepers who kept track of the finances. Their responsibility sometimes included extending workers small amounts of cash. Schroeder's camp office was built in a good vantage spot, south of the river, away from other buildings, overlooking the camp. This building served as the company store and superintendent William Dolan's house. Later, this building became the town of Schroeder's first school. The office generally opened a few hours each evening after supper for the men to pick up their mail, buy new socks, shirts, knives, liniment, mittens, and, their most common purchase, Peerless or Standard tobacco referred to as snuff, snuce or snoose. Theodore Tofte, a North Shore resident, said in a letter, "A man without his snoose could not be expected to do a good day's work. He was apt to be irritable in camp."

Schroeder's camp office.

Woods workers

William Dolan, Schroeder Company superintendent, was an Irishman who, according to Bob Silver, "nobody pushed around." The superintendent needed the respect of the entire organization. Dolan selected the foremen who worked at each camp. W.C. Smith was the foreman at Dam 4, on the main stem of the Cross River, where he lived with his family.

The foremen

The camp foreman oversaw construction and maintenance of camp buildings, laid out logging roads and determined banking and decking areas. Foremen supervised which trees were cut and where they fell. Trees landing in the right place minimized brush cutting and made log removal easier. Foremen instructed sawyers to cut Cross River pines two feet longer than the standard 16-foot length to compensate for damage to the logs as they tumbled down the falls. Battered, splintered, round-butted logs could have stones imbedded in their ends. Stones could endanger mill workers and their saws.

Sawyers

Sawyers had a fairly straightforward job. First they notched a tree with an axe. Then two sawyers worked together, one pulling the cross-cut saw back after his partner pulled it away from him. Reports indicate that two sawyers could cut as many as 100 average-size white pine trees each day.

Each Schroeder camp had at least 12 crews. Usually two crews worked within calling distance of each other. The woods crew cut, limbed, decked and hauled logs. Deckers stacked logs parallel to each other, tier-upon-tier, so they could easily be rolled into the water when the log drive began. At the right time, one strategic sledgehammer blow sent logs into fast-moving water.

Generally a crew had two sawyers, one swamper, one teamster or skidder and a decker. Each crew kept track of their daily work. They knew how much they'd cut and the amount of money they had coming. At the end of each day, logs were measured at landings by scalers. They estimated the number of board feet of lumber in a log using a ruler, also called a cheat stick. To measure, the cheat stick was positioned across the small end (diameter) of the log to read the number of board feet. A 16-inch diameter log in 16-foot lengths, scaled 144 board feet— a 28-incher scaled 576 feet—a 36-incher scaled 1,024 feet.

Swampers

Swampers cleared brush around roads, skidding paths, banking grounds and landings. They used straight-handled, double-bitted axes to cut limbs off felled trees. It was important that all limbs were cut close to the main log to minimize the danger of limbs hitting other workers. Swampers

Courtesy The Vivian Johnson Collection

According to Bob Silver, the lady standing next to the sluiceway is Miss McGrath, who was the Schroeder Company's first school teacher.

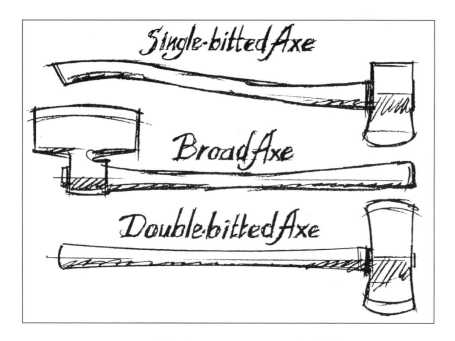

Single-bitted Axe

Broad Axe

Double-bitted Axe

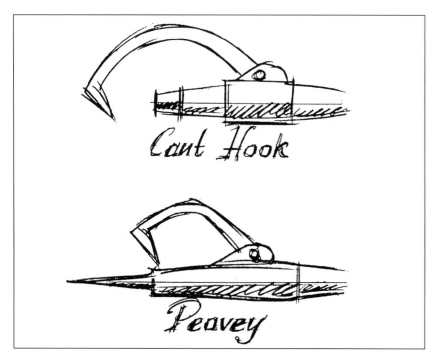

Cant Hook

Peavey

kept roads clean, removed manure, repaired chipped ice and shoveled sand or straw on the tracks in downhill ruts to slow down sleighs.

Teamsters or skidders

Teamsters or skidders used horses to transport logs from where they were cut to landing areas and rollways on frozen waterways. Teamsters wrapped chains around the front end of the log, which rose as the animals pulled, while the back end of the log dragged. Horses snaked and skidded logs to landings a distance of a mile or less. If the distance was greater, logs were piled and restacked on sleighs. Swampers and teamsters worked together, one standing on the sleigh positioning logs with a cant hook, while the other helped guide the logs. Logs were stacked on sleighs 15 to 20 feet high and held in place with heavy chains.

Pulling heavy loads

In order for the horses to pull these heavy loads, logging sleighs had runners on each side. Grooves were made into the iced roads or skidways eight feet apart and six inches deep. The grooves were deep enough so the runners wouldn't jump the tracks. Each night a sleigh hauled large wooden barrels filled with water. These barrels had holes in the bottom, and a twin stream of water went directly into the road ruts.

Cant hook

Also called a cant dog, a cant hook is a free-moving hook hinged to a ring attached to a straight $4\frac{1}{2}$-foot handle. It was used to push, turn and pull logs, providing leverage for stacking and piling. When it hit a log at the proper angle, it bit into it.

Peavey

The peavey, invented in 1858 by Joseph Peavey, a blacksmith, is similar to a cant hook. It has a 5½-foot wooden handle and a free-swinging hook. Its sharp steel point was used to turn, maneuver and prod logs when loading sleighs and for log drives. The steel-tipped point provided leverage between logs caught in a jam. During a log drive, men used it to hook banked or lost logs and pull them into the main flow of water.

Pike pole

The pike pole is a 12-foot pole with a sharp pointed pick at one end, similar to a peavey. It was used to control floating logs. Men would use the sharp point to grab logs, to push and pull them around and to keep them headed straight down the river.

Timber stamps

Each stacked log was hit on its butt end with a hammer that had a cast-steel die imprinted with Schroeder's ownership identification mark. These marks were registered with the State Surveyor of Logs. Brand marks sank deep into the grain and helped settle disputes over log ownership. Some companies had several brands to signify where and when logs were cut.

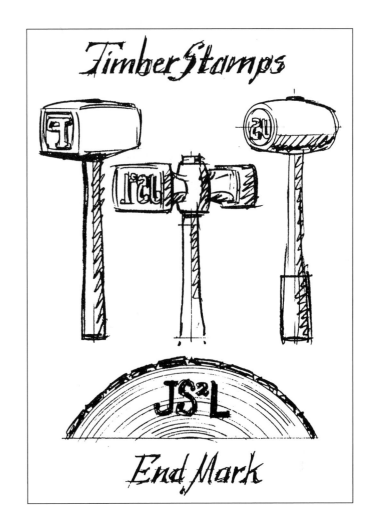

Timber Stamps

End Mark

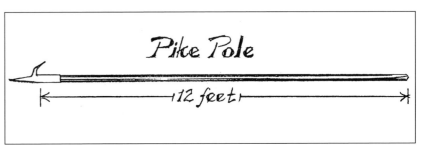

Pike Pole

12 feet

The Cross River before it was dynamited.

How the Cross River was logged

Schroeder started constructing dams in the Cross River watershed and its tributaries in the fall of 1895. Dams impounded water in areas ordinarily not deep enough for logs to float. These wooden dams were 12 to 16 feet high with gates that could be winched open. The largest dam, 6½ miles upstream, was 100 feet long and 14 feet high with three gates. Over the years, as loggers worked in different areas, a total of seven dams were built and numbered in sequence.

Wooden sluiceways (also called sheers or chutes) were constructed in many places on both sides of the river. Sluiceways channeled logs so they would flow straight down the river.

The Cross River drops about 200 feet in the last mile before it enters Lake Superior. Prior to Schroeder's logging operation, the river narrowed and made a sharp bend just before the top of the falls. To be able to use the Cross River, Schroeder dynamited 20 feet off the top of the waterfall. This blast rerouted and widened the river.

The drive

In February 1902, Superintendent Dolan reported that nearly 35,000 average trees equaling 20 million feet of logs were stacked next to the river banks throughout winter and were ready to be brought down. Enough ice and snow had melted and the water had backed up more than a mile behind the largest dam. There was enough water to get logs to the lake. Conditions for the log drive were ideal.

At Dam No. 1, men cranked up the gate winches and let some water run through. Because logs could outrun water, or if the water receded too quickly, logs were apt to get stranded or jam. If the water ran too fast and created too much pressure, it could break Dam No. 2 further downstream. The decker hit the stacked logs with a sledgehammer and the logs tumbled into the water. The men completely opened the first gate. The momentum of water filled with large white pine rushing toward the next dam created a tense situation. If a dam broke, all hell could break loose—jams, people hurt, logs lost. Excitement built as the log drive became reality. Imagine the sound of logs tumbling end over end down the waterfall. It must have been deafening. Bob Silver said his parents heard the drive at their farm seven miles away.

Schroeder used one of Minnesota's earliest telephone systems to coordinate its river drive. By 1897, the telephone line came from the dock at the mouth of the river upstream to the first dam. This battery-operated system connected men at each dam so they knew what was happening in the river and could coordinate the opening and closing of gates to regulate the flow of water. It was a great asset to help avoid jams. Prior to the Schroeder telephone system, the length of time between opening the gates was determined by calculating the speed of the current by throwing a board in the water and timing it for a mile.

Cats on logs

Men who worked the river drives were called "cats on logs." They steered logs and kept them from piling and jamming with peaveys and pike poles. This was dangerous work. If a man happened to be washed into the water, there wasn't much hope for him. Swiftly moving logs knocked more than one cat off a log.

When a jam occurred, logs were pushed and pulled back into the main current. Generally one or two key logs held a jam, and when these were removed, the jam came apart. When jams broke loose, both logs and men moved fast. Men had to react quickly to reach safety. When large log jams formed, dynamite was considered the safest and most effective tool for breaking them up.

When logs finally reached the lake, they were contained in a holding boom. When the drive was done, a few men followed behind in a boat

Courtesy The Schroeder Area Historical Society

The Cross River after it was dynamited.

Calks— (Varying lengths)

Calked Boot

Men who worked on top of logs on the river drive or those that top-loaded logs had pointed calks screwed into their boot soles. This helped them be more surefooted, grip with their feet and minimize slipping on wet logs. Calks were also called spikes or corks and came in different lengths.

called a bateau. They carried peaveys and pike poles to dislodge any logs caught along the way. About a half-mile from Lake Superior, just above the canyon, the men pulled their bateau out of the water. A teamster picked up the bateau, loaded it on a wagon and took it back to the first dam. Bob Silver said, "The old timers told me they had two bateaus on this operation." When water levels behind the dams built up again, the process was repeated and more logs were sent down the river.

Logging was dangerous business, with trees falling, loads shifting, huge logs rushing downstream in fast-moving water in harsh weather. Men were often caught in dangerous situations, took chances and died. Old pictures of the town of Schroeder and personal dairies suggest there was a cemetery south of the river's mouth.

Schroeder completed logging the Cross River in 1905, then sold its interests and facilities to the Alger Smith Lumber Company of Duluth. Most of the men working in the woods returned home to their families and farms. The Schroeder Company packed its cooking equipment and stoves, left the cabins to the woods, but took the doors, frames and windows to be used at the next camp and moved from Cross River to the Apostle Islands. Some men followed Schroeder to work in the Apostle Islands; some chose to work the summer in the Ashland mill.

The Schroeder Company continued to contract for logs with local independent contractors until 1928. Ted Tofte said his father, Andrew, along with his twin brother, John, sold spruce, some pine and a small proportion of poplar and balsam logs to the Schroeder Company for more than 20 years. The Tofte Brothers conducted the last Cross River log drive in 1911.

A telephone conversation at Dam No. 4 between Dolan & Smith

Performed by Clarence Smith and Bob Silver at the Cook County Centennial Celebration on July 27, 1974.

Dolan: Rings phone. One long, one short. No answer. Rings again.

Smith: Hello, Dam 4. Pete talking.

Dolan: Pete, Dolan here. Say Pete, we only have about half a boom full of logs and I was wondering what's the hold-up?

Smith: We had a jam start to develop on that curve south of here in Section 22, so I had Johnson get on it at daylight this morning with a dozen men. It wasn't too bad, but I closed the gates here until they got it cleared. There was a bad rock in there—he's going to blast it out. He should be back most anytime.

Dolan: Well, you know what that Captain is like on the *Ashland*. He sure don't believe in waiting and he ought to be getting in here sometime this evening so he can raft out first thing in the morning when it's calm.

Smith: Yeah, I know. Tell him to be patient. Say, Dolan, remember that quarter-section you said the Company was going to pick up in Section 10 with all that pine on it?

Dolan: Sure do.

Smith: Did the Company ever get the timber-rights on it as we're cutting right along the east side of Section 9 now, and it'd be an easy chance to cut and water those logs this summer. As you know, it's a downhill skid and dray haul, and a good sharp roll off the bank at the river.

Dolan: I haven't had the go-ahead on it yet, but I'll send a note on this to the office with the tug, to remind them.

Smith: Say, Dolan, what ever happened to the fly dope you were going to send up? We have been mixing up bacon grease and kerosene but these Cross River bugs seem to get fat on it. Sure wish you could get hold of some of that Michigan dope in those red cans. That was always pretty good.

Dolan: The tug is supposed to have some fly dope for the horses and the men both, so it will be with the tote team as soon as it gets here. Anything else you need up there?

Smith: Throw on some of those five-foot Peavey handles and some Number 7 and 8 horseshoes. We have plenty of nails and calks. Say, Dolan, I haven't been able to get through on the phone to Dam 6 so I sent Laveck out to walk the line. Maybe another moose caught his horns on the wire like the one did on the line going into 7. We never did find one of the poles and a couple hundred feet of wire.

Dolan: Could be. Keep on that line until you get it in order as we may have to have that water in 6 to fill this raft.

Smith: Dolan, as you know, none of the men came out for the Fourth, so they have been wondering if they could take off Saturday and come to the shore.

Dolan: Since when is Saturday a holiday? *Ashland* needs logs and with pretty good water in the river, we better keep those logs moving. We usually get a dry-spell in August—they'll get a break then.

Smith: Johnson just got in and he said the logs have all been freed at that bend, so I'll get these gates open. Will keep them open until I hear from you. Bye.

Dolan: Good. I'll be talking to you.

CHAPTER TWO

Log Rafting

Logs reached the lake

When logs ended their tumble down the Cross River, they were caught in a holding boom at the river's mouth. Like a corral, this special fence was made of logs chained together. These chained logs, called boom sticks, prevented the logs coming down the river from escaping into Lake Superior. Schroeder used 30-inch by 20-foot white pine logs for boom sticks. Most pine is buoyant. A six-inch hole was cut through each boom log one foot from the end. A 1½ inch iron chain was passed through this hole and threaded through a hole in another boom stick. The chain ends were shackled or riveted together. Boom sticks were linked together end-to-end until their total length was enough to encircle the quantity of cut timber to be rafted across Lake Superior to Ashland, Wisconsin. Over time, Sitka spruce logs shipped in from the West coast replaced the white pine boom sticks. The average rafting boom had 450 boom sticks, three to four feet in diameter and 16 to 22 feet long. A boom made up of 690 boom sticks could contain 6 million board feet of logs.

Metal mooring rings held the boom

Holes were drilled along Lake Superior's bedrock shore and cement docks and 2-foot shafts were placed in each hole. Large metal retaining rings, called mooring rings, were welded to each shaft. At the end of each holding boom, a simple large hook kept booms securely in place. As logs filled it, the holding boom was pushed out further into the lake. "To get more logs into the holding boom, horses pulled one side of the boom and walked with it down the beach," Bob Silver recalled.

Logs were transferred to a rafting boom

When the holding boom was full, logs were transferred into a rafting boom. A winch at the back of a tugboat let out a three-inch steel cable that had an end-hook. The end-hook was attached at the prow of the log

W. C. Smith's fish shanty was near the first wooden bridge (top left) at the mouth of the Cross River.

A string of logs, called boom sticks were held together end-to-end by large iron chains.

Mary Bell at Sugarloaf Cove holding a metal mooring ring.

Tug captains watched over their rafts like a cat watches a mouse.

raft, where three or four logs were fastened together side-to-side with chains to form a platform. This platform had to be strong enough to endure the strain of the log raft being pulled through the water by the tug.

When the log raft was finally made up, a second set of boom log sticks was pulled around it. The outside boom was larger than the inside. In bad weather, logs that escaped the inside boom were caught by the outer strand. This double-stranding technique kept log loss to a minimum. Once a log raft was securely attached to the tug, it was pulled out about a mile into the lake, and all the lines were checked and tightened. After three or four hours of being pulled, the log raft formed a teardrop shape. Rafts appeared to shrink as they were pulled, because the cluster of logs got tighter. Ed Erickson referred to this as "loving up." Once under way, rafts could withstand a terrific pounding from wind and water without breaking up.

Tugs move out into the lake

After 34 miles of pulling a log raft across open water in the largest of the Great Lakes, tugs reached the protection of the most westerly Apostle Island, Sand Island. The destination was the Schroeder mill in Ashland. Traveling at one mile per hour, a tug generally took three days to pull a log raft the 72 miles across Lake Superior from Cross River to Ashland.

A typical raft tug was from 120 to 150 feet long and about 30 feet wide. Its hull was made of white oak. Cabins were made of pine. Its steam boiler was fueled with coal. Tugs had lights, whistles and steam horns. They did not have radar or radios. They watched for lighthouse beams and listened for fog horn signals. Careful watch of the compass kept them on course.

The large, double-decked tugs that pulled rafts across the lake were often accompanied by a small tug about 50 feet in length, called a tender. The tender's crew rode herd on the raft, ran errands and responded to emergencies. It was a flexible vessel, like a harbor tug, that could even ride over boom sticks.

A different kind of June bugs

In order to keep track of the raft throughout the night and to warn off other vessels, kerosene lanterns were placed on boom stick platforms. These lights were referred to as June bugs. One was directly behind the tug at the far end of the raft; the other two were placed at 90-degree angles to the first light. Each afternoon, the raftsman took the tender back to the raft to refuel and light the lanterns.

Weather played a significant role

Lake Superior has a treacherous reputation. Rafting usually began after the ice melted and the spring storms had passed, sometimes as early as mid-April. Fred Mackie remembered summer rafting as generally smooth, with two- to five-foot waves. "By late July," Mackie said, "winds blew earlier and stronger each day, and by mid-August the lake got rough. By September, storms were more likely, and Lake Superior in a howling northeaster was truly awesome." Bob Silver describes the lake's unforgiving ways: "Lake Superior says, 'I'll let you go this time, but I'll teach you a good lesson next time.'"

Pulling a raft was tricky business

Slow to start, hard to stop, pulling a log raft was tricky business. Tugs headed directly into the wind, otherwise sidewinds could break rafts apart. Strong winds could blow a tug and its raft backward. Rafts of several million board feet withstood storms better than smaller rafts. During a storm, when the force of huge waves struck against a large raft, the front logs piled up and the rest of the raft was less affected.

Ed Erickson has logged, fished and boated on Lake Superior all his life and knows the Apostle Islands very well.

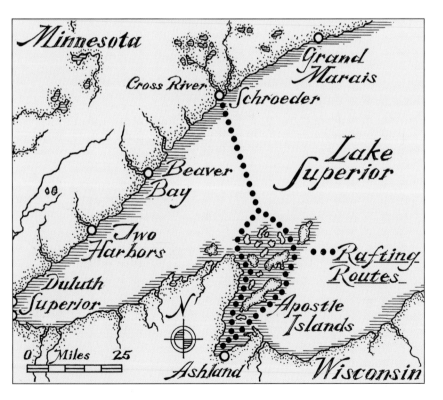

Lake Superior

Lake Superior is 350 miles across east to west and 160 miles north to south. This freshwater lake has 2,980 miles of shoreline enclosing 2,935 cubic miles of water and covers 31,700 square miles (⅔ in the United States and ⅓ in Canada). Just north of Munising, Michigan, Lake Superior reaches a depth of 1,333 feet.

Schroeder rafts

Schroeder's log rafts were relatively small, therefore rafting started early in the spring in order to get enough logs to the mill so it could run continuously. Over the years, more powerful tugs pulled larger rafts and reduced the risk of encountering stormy weather. With larger rafts, the rafting season was reduced to 12 to 14 weeks, generally early June through mid-September.

In April 1902, the Ashland Daily Press reported, "Fifty Million Feet Estimated on The North Shore—The Season Will Begin Early." As a general rule, May 15 was the first feasible date to start log rafting. The newspaper went on to report, "The hastening of operations is due to the season being practically a month earlier than usual due to the anxiety of loggers to get their timber to the sawmills. All depends on the weather, as it does at any time along the North Shore. If the prevailing wind is off shore, or if there is no particular blow, log-shore operators think their chances are as good for obtaining good weather as if they waited until May, but very unfavorable weather has prevailed so far on account of the strong winds. Last year, an effort was made to tow logs in May, but very unfavorable weather prevailed the early part of the season, well up until August. Some big tug and labor bills were incurred while tugs and crews were on 'lay time' waiting for weather. A number of rafts got caught in northeasters and were slammed up against the rocks, breaking boom sticks apart and scattering logs up and down the shore. It is claimed, that by exercise, care and vigilance of the tug captain, a raft can be made to weather a pretty fierce northeaster down the shore, if it's pulled away from the beach in time. There is said to be very little danger of a raft breaking or spilling a very large proportion of its logs unless it's banged up against rocks. A tow line may break or boom chains give away, but losses from these causes have not been as numerous as those where the raft was kept too near the shore. It's said to be due to the ambition of those having charge of rafting, to get as much timber in the water as possible, even after a blow has come up, rather than starting when it's too late to get away from the shore in the face of a heavy northeaster."

Schroeder's first 800,000-foot raft from Cross River arrived at the Ashland mill on June 11, 1902. As soon as the tug pulled the raft into port, the raft was dumped into the mill pond. The tug took on supplies, got coal from the dock; the crew washed clothes, got back on board and the tug headed back out across the lake. Once under way, the boom sticks were pulled together to make long parallel lines that floated behind the tug. These long lines allowed the tug to travel faster as it went across the lake to get another log raft.

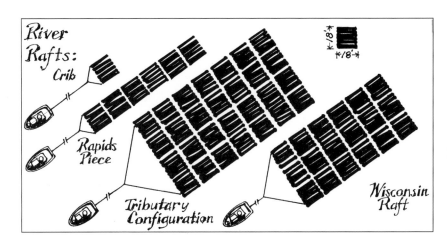

River rafting was different from lake rafting

Logs were rafted on lakes, and lumber was rafted on rivers. To raft lumber, cribs were built at the lumber mill on platforms called cradles. A crib was 18-by-18 feet square. When a crib was loaded with cut lumber, it was tilted, slid off the cradle and ready to float down the river. It could take weeks to get a river raft downstream. River rafts were generally tied to the shore at night. A shack on the raft served as the cookhouse. As the raft floated on the current, oarsmen kept it in channels, clear of sand bars and other dangers.

Sugarloaf Cove

From the late 1800s through the early 1900s, log rafting took place at the mouth of many North Shore rivers and streams. The busiest and longest-lived raft assembly landing was Sugarloaf Cove. Sugarloaf Cove is 73 miles northeast of Duluth and eight miles southwest of the town of Schroeder. Its name comes from the loaflike rocky point that projects out into the lake that looked like loaves of sugar sold in a general goods store. This natural harbor provided shelter and protection for the assembly of log rafts.

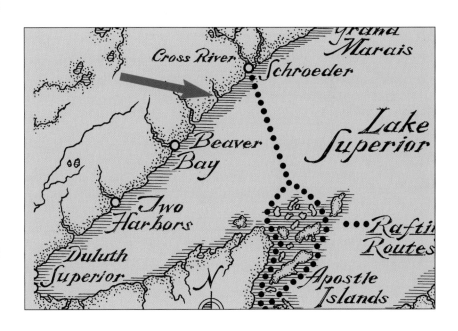

Aerial photograph of making a raft at Sugarloaf Cove.

Most people, however, believe Sugarloaf Cove was never used by the Schroeder Company to assemble log rafts. Bob Hagman, former Consolidated Paper Company District Superintendent, remembers, "The boom shafts and rings at Sugarloaf were made of lightweight, ¼-inch steel—the style used for the earlier, smaller log rafts. In fact, Consolidated replaced these shafts with larger shafts and rings." It should be noted that over the years many commercial fishermen who utilized Sugarloaf Cove used these boom shafts to secure their vessels to the shore. These shafts may have belonged to them. It's also true that the Schroeder Company and Consolidated Paper had close business ties in Ashland for many years.

Each fall and winter, Consolidated Paper cut spruce, jack pine and balsam. Pulpwood logs were cut in eight-foot lengths in comparison to logs for lumber which were cut 16 feet long. Tractors hauled pulpwood logs to a staging area. They were cut and trucked to Sugarloaf where they were stacked. Cranes transferred the logs to trucks that dumped them down an 80-foot chute and into the cove. Three or four times each season, logs were assembled into rafts that covered many acres.

Life on a tug

Although the *Butterfield* was not a Schroeder tug, Fred Mackie's experiences as a deckhand and fireman on the vessel provide insight into what it was like to work and live on a tug. The *Butterfield* brought pulpwood rafts from Ontario, Canada's Nipigon River, the Pigeon River in Minnesota and various North Shore locations to Ashland.

An average tug had a crew of eight to 12 hard-working men. They wore blue work shirts, jeans, heavy shoes, gloves and always a cap. The firemen, deckhands and oilers slept in the prow under the main deck in a bunk about 30 inches wide and 6 feet long, with just enough space to sit up. "At all times you could feel the vibrating engines," Mackie said. "If you didn't feel them, it meant something was wrong, and you got out of bed fast." The engineers, captain, mate and wheelsmen slept on the deck above. Hot showers were always available because the engine heated water.

Control was in the captain's hands and he was always on duty. If anything went wrong, he was responsible for all the decisions. His turn on watch was six hours on and six hours off.

The first mate rotated time on and off with the captain. He was a captain-in-training. His position was similar to a foreman in a logging camp. He had responsibility over the crew. In 1951, a mate earned about $230 a month.

The chief engineer was the engine room boss. Tug engines were always in need of supervision and adjustment. The assistant engineer alternated with the chief engineer, six hours on and six hours off.

Three firemen worked four hours on and eight hours off. In 1930 each was paid about $70 a month. They worked hard, constantly feeding soft (bituminous) coal in and shoveling ashes out. "In summer," Mackie recalled, "it got pretty warm down in the fire hole. Feeding coal was dirty, dusty, hard work."

The galley crew had two members—a cook and a porter. "Food on a tug was always good," Mackie said. "In fact, all lake boats were famous for good food because they traveled from urban areas where supplies were accessible." On smaller tugs, the cook also served as a deckhand.

Two deckhands did routine cleaning, moored lines and helped the firemen. They worked six hours on and six hours off. In 1930, they made $50 to $60 a month. By 1951, they made about $100.

Three oilers worked in the engine room. They kept the engine lubricated to prevent it from seizing up. It was a cleaner job than that of firemen. Oilers worked four hours on and eight hours off. They were paid about $80 a month in the 1930s.

Courtesy The Mary Bell Collection

Fred Mackie was a deckhand on the tug Butterfield *during the summers of 1929 and 1930, and from 1931 to 1933 he was one of its firemen.*

Pat Labadie has been director of the United States Army Corps of Engineer's Lake Superior's Visitor Center in Duluth, Minnesota, since 1973. He made it possible to retrieve and reproduce information about these Lake Superior vessels.

Two wheelsmen worked in the pilot house, steering the tug. They rotated six hours on and six hours off and earned $90 a month.

The tug had one raftsman, whose job was to tend to the raft. He was on duty all the time. He was not really a part of the ship's crew. "If something went wrong, he and the captain worked it out," Mackie noted.

Mackie recalled a story about the time a man got lost. "One night, just out of Ashland, on the tug *Ashland,* on the way to Outer Island, a member of the crew fell asleep on the fantail at the back of the tug. In the morning, he was nowhere to be found. He fell off during the night."

Schroeder vessels

The Schroeder Company owned and leased tugs, steam barges and scows on Lake Superior. The scows hauled logs, lumber and supplies. Steamers hauled lumber through the locks at Sault Saint Marie to the Schroeder lumber yards in Milwaukee. Schroeder vessels delivered lumber as far east as North Tonawanda, near Buffalo, New York, which is 939 nautical miles from Ashland.

According to United States Army Corps of Engineers records in Duluth, Minnesota, the Schroeder Company owned the *A. C. Van Raalte,* (renamed the *Ashland*), the *Saugatuck,* the *Henry F. Brower* and the *John Schroeder.* They leased the *George E. Brockway,* the *J. C. Ames,* the *E. G. Crosby* and the *Traveler.* The *Hilton,* a steamer, was used to transport lumber. Although Schroeder never used the tug *Butterfield,* it's included in this text because it was an extraordinary tug with a rich, colorful, informative history and the pride of Ashland. Schroeder owned two scows, the *Bob Cook* and the *Finn McCool.* References suggest the Schroeder Company also used the *W. H. Sawyer, T. S. Christie, Louis Pahlow* and the *Niko* to haul lumber and to tow barges.

Courtesy U.S. Army Corps of Engineers, Duluth, Minnesota

Official U. S. #1496: Length 87.4 feet—Width 19.6 feet

A. C. Van Raalte / Ashland

Schroeder bought the *A. C. Van Raalte* tug from the Nester Lumber Company in 1901. In August 1903 it was renamed the *Ashland.* This big tug had a tremendous capacity to pull. It was built in 1867 in Buffalo, New York, by Hitchcock & Gibson. Its engine was built by Sheriffs Manufacturing Company the same year. Originally it was a passenger propeller. In 1899, it was turned into a tug. A Captain LaChapelle piloted it for many years. On June 2, 1903, the *Van Raalte* was towing a 500,000-foot log raft from the North Shore when a piston rod broke its engine. It was rescued by another tug that towed it and the log raft to Ashland. The Schroeder Company leased the tug *George E. Brockway* while it was being repaired. In July, 1907, the tug *Crosby* towed the disabled tug *Ashland* to drydock in Superior, Wisconsin, where it was almost completely rebuilt during the winter of 1908.

Van Raalte/Ashland activity log

The following two-year activity log exemplifies what a typical rafting tug accomplished. Although impressive, it's not a complete listing of all the rafts brought to Ashland or all the trips made.

1901
- May 10, delivered to Ashland the first 1 million board-foot log raft from the Baptism River on the North Shore.
- May 21, the fourth log raft arrived from the North Shore. Four of the 7 million feet of logs arrived in Ashland with the rest expected by June 1.
- June 4, the last of the 7 million feet arrived, a 1.2 million log raft with W. H. Gilbert's logs consigned to Schroeder.
- June 27, a 900,000-foot log raft, containing some of Nester's lost logs.
- July 12, boom sticks were brought from Duluth.
- Aug 5, an 800,000-foot log raft from Iron River, Michigan.
- October 4, returned from taking camp supplies to the North Shore.

1902
- More rafts were towed from the Minnesota shore this season than ever before. The Ashland harbor estimated an increase of 200 vessels.
- April 14, a log raft from Red Cliff.
- April 18, a 1.4 million-foot log raft from Bayfield.
- June 11, a 800,000-foot log raft from the Cross River.
- June 17, 1 million-foot log raft.
- July 1, a log raft from the Cross River.
- July 14, a 1.5 million-foot log raft from the Cross River.
- July 18, two Georgian Bay log booms, each with 800 boom sticks from Sault Saint Marie.
- Aug 11, a 3 million-foot log raft from the North Shore.
- Aug 23, 100,000 feet of hemlock from Madeline Island.
- Sept 26, delivered 14 horses and logging supplies to the North Shore.
- Oct 11, a 1 million-foot log raft from Iron River.
- October, a 1.5 million-foot log raft from the Cross River.

Heavy water

"North Shore rafting is over for the season. The tugs 'Vigilant' and 'Van Raalte' are the only tugs from Ashland delivering supplies to the North Shore camps. Neither care to risk being caught out on the lake towing a raft in a storm this late in the season. The water is not only very cold, but it is much heavier than it is earlier in the season and the waves do more damage."

The Ashland Daily Press, November 20, 1902

When making up a log raft, things could go wrong…

"The heavy northeast winds on Lake Superior during the past few days have played havoc with log rafts. The Nester estate, at the time of the big blow on the lake last Friday, was building a huge raft to be towed from the North Shore as the sea rose. Every effort was made to save the logs from going adrift. In spite of all that could be done, within a few hours after the raft went to pieces, the logs were scattered for miles along the shore. Lost logs were valued at $20,000. The lost logs will be retrieved as soon as the sea subsides."

The Ashland Daily Press, June 1901

Courtesy U.S. Army Corps of Engineers, Duluth, Minnesota

Official U. S. #115403: Length 84 feet—Width 17 feet

Saugatuck

The *Saugatuck* was built in 1875 by John B. Martel in Saugatuck, Michigan. The engine was built by Bay City Iron Works in Michigan in 1880. Schroeder bought it on May 20, 1914, and sold it May 29, 1929. It was placed in the Sturgeon Bay, Wisconsin, boneyard in 1930. It was a small rafting tug used in the Apostle Islands and around Ashland. In May 1917, the *Saugatuck* pulled the scow *Bob Cook* loaded with five carloads of steers to the Stockton Island logging camp. On August 10, 1920, it pulled a 9,000-cord pulpwood raft from Grand Marais, Minnesota. This was the last of the largest consignment of American pulpwood logged during the winter of 1920. In July, 1921, it pulled a 2,500-cord pulpwood raft from Grand Marais.

Official U. S. #95694: Length 60 feet—Width 15 feet

Official U. S.#76883: Length 154.8 feet—Width 29.8 feet—Horsepower 555

Henry F. Brower

This small tug was built in 1882. Schroeder bought it in 1915. With Captain Ernie La Pointe at the wheel, it hauled men and supplies to the Schroeder camps in the Apostle Islands and assisted the tug *Ashland.* It was later owned by the Lake Superior Towing Company, and its Captain was Elias Moe.

John Schroeder

The *John Schroeder* was built in 1890 in Sheboygan, Wisconsin, by Riebolt and Water and cost $46,000. Its engine was built by F. L. McGregor in Milwaukee, Wisconsin, and was rebuilt in 1899. This steam barge had the capacity to haul 500,000 board feet of lumber on and below its deck. With 12 to 14 men aboard, its usual destination was Schroeder's Lumber Yard in Milwaukee, Wisconsin. Schroeder sold it in September 1912 to Sydney C. McLouth, Marine City, Michigan. In 1916, it was renamed the *William A. Hazard* and put into the cement trade business. Winkworth Fuel & Transit Company owned it from 1925 through 1933. It was abandoned in 1934 and dismantled and scrapped in Milwaukee, Wisconsin, in November 1937.

Courtesy U.S. Army Corps of Engineers, Duluth, Minnesota

Official U. S. #10666: Length 112 feet—Width 20 feet—Horsepower 804

Courtesy U.S. Army Corps of Engineers, Duluth, Minnesota

Official U. S. #76400: Length 160.2 feet—Width 29 feet—Horsepower 1,000

George E. Brockway

This powerful, well-known vessel was in the same class as the *Ashland* and the *Traveler.* It was built in 1867 in Port Huron, Michigan, by F. C. Leighton. Its high-pressure engine was built in 1867 by the Cuyahoga Furnace Company in Ohio. The Schroeder Company leased the *G. E. Brockway* when the *Van Raalte* suffered engine damage in 1903. It was used to tow a 2 million-foot log raft from Cross River and five rafts, estimated at 10 million feet each, from Sault Saint Marie.

J. C. Ames

According to Pat Labadie, "The *J. C. Ames* was an extraordinarily handsome and powerful towing tug. It was one of the largest, most powerful rafting tugs on the Great Lakes." It was built in 1882 in Manitowoc, Wisconsin, by Rand & Burger at a cost of more than $50,000. Its engine was built by Detroit Dry Dock Company in Michigan. It had electric lights including a searchlight. It was christened the *J. C. Perrett* and owned first by the Marinette Barge Line. From 1885 through 1908, it was owned by the Lake Michigan Car Ferry Company and renamed the *J. C. Ames.* In 1908, the Newaygo Tug Line of Green Bay bought it for $8,000. Because Newaygo Tug Line was a Canadian subsidiary of Consolidated Paper, the *J. C. Ames* was Consolidated's first tug. Along with the tug *Erna,* the *Ames* brought pulpwood rafts from Canada for the Schroeder Company. It was abandoned in 1923 because of its age.

Official U.S. #136320: Length 89 feet—Width 18 feet

Official U. S. #2767: Length 140 feet—Width 24 feet

E. G. Crosby

Although a little larger than a harbor tug, the *E. G. Crosby* was considered small for an open-water tug. Hundreds of this type were used on the Great Lakes. It was built in 1892 in Grand Haven, Michigan, by D. Robertson. Its engine was built in 1892 by Wilson and Hendrie of Montague, Michigan.

Although there is no official record of Schroeder ownership, Schroeder used it to bring rafts from Minnesota to its Ashland mill. The Lake Michigan Car Ferry Transit and the Great Lakes Towing Company were listed as owners. It was abandoned in 1914 and its engine went into the tug *Illinois*.

Traveler

This huge and powerful tug was used to raft logs from Canada to Ashland. First named the *Bismark,* in 1877 it was valued at $20,000. It was renamed the *Justice Field* in 1884 and in 1891 it was rebuilt and named the *Traveler.* "The *Traveler* with its decorative Victorian features was the quintessential tug," Pat Labadie said. It was built in 1871 in Sheboygan, Wisconsin, by Alfred Stokes and John Gregory. *Traveler's* first engine was built in 1856 and installed in a steamer called the *Equator.* In 1871, it was put in the tug *Bismark.* In 1890, it got a new engine built by F. W. Wheeler and Company.

The *Traveler* was seized in a legal dispute in Ashland in September 1915. Before the tug was released, Captain Joseph Marx had to pay a $50 grocery bill.

Bad news–good ending

The tug Traveler sprang a leak and started taking on water during a big storm on Lake Superior on September 25, 1919. Forced to save itself, the tug was 25 miles northeast of Outer Island when the crew cut loose its 6,000 cord pulpwood raft from the North Shore valued at $54,000. The tug was unable to hold the raft in the 60-mile gale. The raft drifted northeast across shipping lanes.

The following summer several tugs helped round up logs that had washed ashore from this raft along 100 miles of coastline. In September 5,000 cords were brought to Ashland. It is more than interesting that between 1919 and 1920 pulpwood prices increased in value about 50 percent because of a shortage. As a result, the Pulpwood Company of Appleton, Wisconsin, actually made more money on this raft, even though they lost 1,000 cords.

The Ashland Daily Press, September 3, 1920

The Traveler *slid off blocks while in drydock in 1919.*

In July 1918, a rumor floated around the Ashland harbor of a possible sale of the *Traveler* to a Seattle, Washington, company. Seattle was a rafting and lumber center and needed tugs as this business grew. The *Traveler* would have traveled down the Great Lakes to the Atlantic, down the coast, through the newly built Panama Canal, then made a sharp turn north to Seattle. But it stayed in Lake Superior.

In 1917, the *Traveler,* owned by Russell Timber Company of Port Arthur, Ontario, Canada, was sold to the Pulpwood Company of Neenah, Wisconsin, and was leased and operated by the Schroeder Company until 1919. In 1918, it beached in the Ashland harbor after hitting sharp ends of a submerged wood pile. It was sent to Duluth's dry docks to get its hull repaired. In 1919, the *Traveler* was sold to Lake Superior Paper Company at Sault Saint Marie. They used it until 1921 when Abitibi Paper Company of Canada bought and rebuilt it and

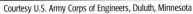

Courtesy U.S. Army Corps of Engineers, Duluth, Minnesota

Official U. S. #11767: Length 110 feet—Width 76.4 feet

renamed it the *G. R. Gray.* They used it to tow rafts along the eastern shore of Lake Superior until September 18, 1937, when it was abandoned in Thessalon, Ontario, and stripped in 1949. Vandals burned it in 1959.

Hilton

This steam barge was built in 1867 at East Saginaw, Michigan. The engine was built by Vulcan Iron Works in Milwaukee in 1867. John Schroeder and C.H. Ellis of Milwaukee are each listed as half owner on April 1, 1896, with John Cook the master. From April 1901 to July 1903, C. H. Ellis was the master. J. A. Murdock became its master in September 1903. In March 1907, the John Schroeder Lumber Company became its owner, with Henry H. Schroeder listed as vice president and

master. Schroeder sold it in 1913 to the Diamond Crystal Salt Company in Detroit. It ended up in Canada.

"The *Hilton* was not only colorful," said Labadie, "it served as a prototype for steam barges. This landmark vessel was among the first in a series of about 800 steam barges on the Great Lakes. It revolutionized the lumber trade by making it financially practical to haul lumber. It was capable of towing as many as five barges or scows. This type of vessel was heavily used until the Great Depression." Schroeder used it to haul scows loaded with hardwood from the Apostle Islands to the Ashland mill, tow log rafts and deliver lumber. In May 1909, the *Hilton* took 18 horses from the Stockton Island camp to Ashland. Starting in September 1909, it made weekly trips, with regular stops at various lakeshore communities, between Duluth and Ontonagon, Michigan, to deliver mail, people and supplies.

45

Aerial view of tug and raft.

Official U. S. #218244: Length 149 feet—Width 28 feet—Horsepower 750

Butterfield

"The *Butterfield*," said Labadie, "was the most popular vessel in the Ashland Harbor. It was a big, impressive tug." It was built in 1919 at Elizabeth, New Jersey, and with its steel hull it was destined for ocean service. Its steam engine was built by Bethlehem Ship Building Company. The *Butterfield* was not owned or operated by Schroeder, but it pulled other companies' rafts to Schroeder's Ashland facilities.

Consolidated Water Power & Paper Company brought the Butterfield to Lake Superior in 1923 to raft pulpwood. It was freshly painted in 1929. From 1929 through 1941, Thomas Mackie was her master and Lewis LaChapelle was a mate. The Butterfield was drafted into service in the Aleutian Islands from 1943 through 1944. After the war, Roen Steamship Company of Sturgeon Bay bought, overhauled, refitted, converted it to diesel power and renamed it the *John Purves* in 1956. Eder Barge & Towing of Milwaukee bought the *John Purves* for $250,000 on April 8, 1974. This vessel is owned by Canonie Marine Transportation and still operates out of East Muskegon, Michigan.

Once lost—now found

On June 30, 1914, a 6,000-cord pulpwood raft headed to Schroeder's Ashland mill from Port Arthur, Canada, broke loose during a severe storm. This $33,000 raft belonged to the Appleton Pulpwood Company. The raft was sighted off Devils Island in the Apostles, although a search of the vicinity found no trace of it. A week later the Lake Superior Towing Company finally found it and towed it to Ashland.

The Butterfield.

Back of the tug.

Courtesy
The Fred Mackie Collection

Fred Mackie as a deck hand.

A roundup

In June 1901, The Nester Lumber Company lost 1.5 million board feet when a raft broke loose in a storm. The Lumber and Log Owners' Association of Bayfield, Ashland and Washburn, Wisconsin, initiated a roundup. Private independent contractors often helped round up lost logs. An estimated 2.5 million feet of stray logs was scattered around Chequamegon Bay and the Apostle Islands. When the logs were recovered, because they were branded, their owners received reimbursement. A log scaler tallied each company's logs. Each owner was paid $5.25 per thousand, which included sawing costs. The independent contractor bought the logs from the lumber companies and any profits, after expenses, they kept.

An Ed Erickson story

Ed Erickson tells the story of a log raft being pulled at night in blinding fog. "Before the captain went to sleep, he looked out and saw leaves on trees on a nearby shore. When he woke at first light, he saw the same leaves on the same trees. What had happened was the raft had gotten too close to the edge of Oak Island and the raft had hooked and wrapped around the island's end. The tug had pulled all night and they never moved. The skipper and the mate wouldn't admit to this, but word got around."

Lost logs

"The Dam at the Mouth of Oronto River's Gone Along With Three Million Feet of Logs—Seven inches of rain fell within 48 hours." This ferocious downpour caused Schroeder's logs to spew into Lake Superior. The steam barge Hilton and several other tugs rushed to the scene to boom the logs. The rescue was unsuccessful and was considered a total loss.

In the same storm, the Stearns Lumber Company was logging nearby on the Bad River and lost 5.5 million feet of logs. However, tugs rescued these logs and towed them to a Washburn, Wisconsin, sawmill.

The Ashland Daily Press, July 22, 1909

Scows

A scow is a type of wooden barge with square ends that sits low in the water. Scows hauled non-floating logs to and lumber from the mill. They also hauled cattle, pigs, horses and supplies to and from Schroeder's Apostle Island camps. Animals had to walk a plank to get off the barge. At the end of the plank they were shoved into the water and they swam to shore.

The *Finn McCool* and the *Bob Cook* were both owned by Schroeder. These identical vessels were 120 feet long and 36 feet wide. The scows changed hands many times, and Ed Erickson of Bayfield was the final owner of them both.

The *Finn McCool* was built in 1907 by Clyde Iron Works of Duluth, Minnesota. Its steam engine was also built by Clyde. It had a steam hoist to load hardwood logs. Its boom was 80 feet long and 14 inches wide and was made of western fir. When the scow was launched, it sprang a leak and had to be reinforced. The *Finn McCool* eventually sank in a boat slip in Bayfield, Wisconsin.

Built in 1907, the *Bob Cook* and the tug *Saugatuck* took carloads of steers to Stockton Island. The *Bob Cook* sits underwater in Bayfield harbor about 800 feet from the *Finn McCool*, with a corner sticking out above the water.

A rafting incident

By Fred Mackie

In September 1930, the sixth and largest raft of the season, 17,000 cords of pulpwood, left Black Bay, Ontario, headed for Ashland. This 300-mile trip generally took a tug 10 to 12 days to pull a log raft. The *Butterfield* was assisted by two smaller Canadian tugs, the *James Whalen* and *Puckasaw* from Port Arthur. The *Dispatch* was the *Butterfield's* tender.

It was late in the season to raft logs across the lake. The captain estimated it would take six days of really good weather to reach the shelter of the Apostles. They skirted the North Shore of Isle Royale. Then, leaving behind Isle Royale's Rock of Ages lighthouse, they started across the 70 miles of open water to the Apostles. A stiff northeast wind began two days out of Isle Royale. The Captain, Tom Mackie, my uncle, was worried, they were being blown off course toward the west. He realized they would pass west of Outer Island instead of east of it. Beyond Outer Island and to the west were the rocky cliffs of Devils Island. Captain Mackie ordered a change of course to compensate for the wind. He turned into the wind (east-northeast); although losing headway, he gained time and slowly drifted south. That night, they saw the Outer Island lighthouse about seven miles away. The only possible shelter from the northeast wind was Michigan Island, 15 miles to the south. South of Outer Island was Stockton Island with its expansive sandy beaches.

The tugs strained against the wind and waves throughout the next day. The *Puckasaw* pushed from behind while the *Whalen* pulled. By late afternoon, the two small tugs were in distress, having more trouble staying afloat than doing their share of towing. Finally, the two smaller tugs cut loose from the log raft and headed for shelter at Stockton Island.

The wind continued to push the *Butterfield* and the log raft back toward Stockton Island. Captain Mackie knew he wouldn't make the shelter of Michigan Island and decided to drift back into the big bay on the northeast side of Stockton Island. He was successful in his attempt, and the raft came to rest on the sandy beach. The *Butterfield* let go of the raft and headed for shelter until the storm passed. When the storm abated, the *James Whalen* went to Ashland for help. The tug *Ashland* responded. All tugs hooked onto the raft, pulled it off the beach and towed it to the Ashland storage boom. Most of the raft remained intact. Only about 1,000 cords were lost. This raft, one of the largest spruce pulpwood rafts ever towed, approximately 8.5 million feet, covered an area the size of three to four football fields.

CHAPTER THREE

Logging the Apostle Islands

Logging made a tremendous impact on the Apostle Islands

The relatively small Apostle Islands were dense with trees. All logging took place fairly close to water. Logs did not have to be hauled great distances. Ravines and gullies became chutes to get logs down to the lake. In winter, ice and snow provided smooth ruts for sleighs to get logs to the staging area. After spring breakup, softwood logs were rafted and hardwoods were brought on scows to the Ashland mill. Each scow could carry as much as 100,000 board feet per load.

Cutting white pine in the islands began around 1860. Schroeder logged white pine, hardwoods, cedar, hemlock and pulpwood on Stockton, Oak, Michigan and Outer islands from 1909 to 1931. At first, hardwoods were cut for fuel, then for lumber. White pine was the preferred building material. Cedar became fence posts and shingles. Hemlock bark was peeled off in 12- to 18-inch strips four to five feet long for the tanbark industry. The peeled logs were cut for lumber. Eventually pulpwood became paper, plywood and particle board.

Logging was a lonely business

Although commercial fishermen frequented the islands and lighthouse attendants lived on some islands, lumberjacks were isolated. Men worked from 6 a.m. to 6 p.m., six days a week. In winter, when they finally got a day off, there was no place to go. Weather and ice conditions limited mainland access. When the lake was navigable, tugs and scows brought supplies, equipment and animals, but in the cold of winter, men were entirely dependent on stored supplies and each other for company. Schroeder used tugs and scows to transport steers and pigs to Stockton and Oak Islands. In April 1915, it was documented that 200 steers were let loose on Oak Island and about 600 more in May 1917. They ran wild, fattened up at no cost and provided a continuous supply of fresh meat.

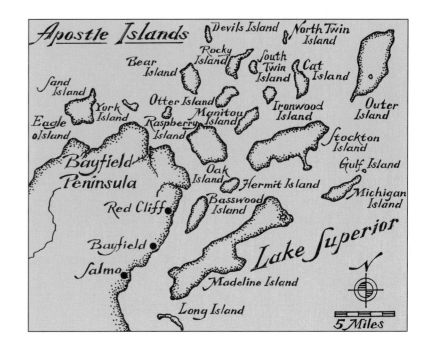

Courtesy The Mary Bell Collection

Big wheels were the summer alternative to winter skidding. Logs were raised, one end was chained to the big wheel's axle and the back end of the log dragged on the ground to the lake.

Marooned men

Almost 100 men marooned on Stockton Island for nearly two weeks sent one man on a daring two-mile trip across rotting ice and floating bergs between Stockton and Madeline islands on April 20, 1916. When this adventurous soul reached Madeline Island, he called Ashland for help. (Madeline Island got telephones in the summer of 1915.) The tug Ashland broke through the ice and took all the men to the mainland.

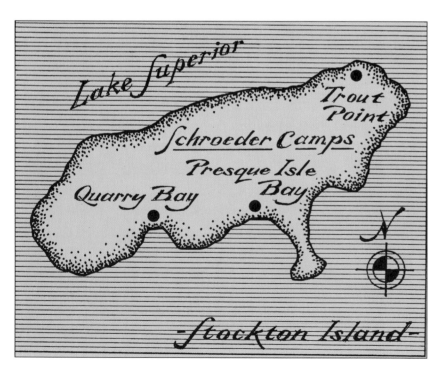

Medical attention was important

Schroeder generally employed a company doctor to take care of men working on the islands from late fall until early spring. When the water was open, the tug took Ashland doctors to the camps. One year, when Schroeder didn't have a doctor, Lyle Murdock, the son of J. A. Murdock, Schroeder's Presque Island camp superintendent, became sick on Stockton Island. The Schroeder crew staged a strike until a resident doctor was brought to the island. When loggers were injured, fellow workers often quit their jobs, not wanting to work in a place where medical attention was limited.

Stockton Island

Stockton is the second-largest Apostle Island. Its 10,000 acres are about seven miles long and 2½ miles wide. About 40 miles from Ashland, it's one of the loveliest islands, with a stone quarry, a bog, lagoon, long beaches and picturesque caves. William King cut hardwoods, pine and hemlock on Stockton Island in the 1880s and 1890s. By 1905, Schroeder had a 12-year lease with William Vilas of the Superior Lumber Company of Ashland for "all trees and timber of every kind and nature" on Stockton Island. Schroeder paid all taxes on the leased land. Trout Point, Presque Isle Bay and Quarry Bay were logged between 1909 and 1920. By 1915, the Stockton Island camps were a major part of Schroeder's logging operation, employing 100 to 250 men.

Trout Point Camp

Schroeder's Trout Point Camp at Stockton Island's northern tip was 22 miles across the water from Bayfield. In winter it was unsafe to cross the ice, so the camp stocked large amounts of supplies. Schroeder constructed logging buildings, built roads, railroads, trams, wharves and docks. This winter sleigh-haul, company-operated camp operated from 1915 through 1918.

William King first cut white pine here. Frederick Prentice of the Excelsior Brownstone Company cut white pine and hemlock in 1890. E. K. Brigham cut hemlock and hardwood in 1907. In December 1908 Brigham sold his interest and logging outfit to J. B. Matthews, who employed about 60 men.

Archeological surveys have identified eight structures including two bunkhouses, a kitchen, dining hall, a root cellar with double-walled construction, a filers shack, camp store, stable and blacksmith shop, plus several earthen embankments, drainage ditches, privies and logs.

Presque Isle Bay Camp

This camp sits on a bank above a long sandy beach on the north side of Presque Isle Bay. This clearing was one of the largest and most protected areas on any of the islands. It provided easy lake access and was a major log staging area.

William King logged pine here in the 1880s. In 1891, William Vilas owned most of Stockton Island. In 1902, Schroeder leased it from Vilas and logged hardwoods and hemlock from 1915 through 1919. This Schroeder campsite still contains several building foundations, dump areas and dock cribs. From the air, a network of drainage ditches is visible. An east-west trail runs through the camp.

Quarry Bay Logging Camp

William Vilas and John Knight owned this site in 1898. Schroeder took over in the early 1900s and logged hemlock and hardwoods. Quarry Bay was the main camp. As many as 12 structures have been identified along with dump areas and a pit of sawn cattle bones. The dock still provides a mooring place for boaters. This sheltered bay provided an excellent South Shore landing area.

The logging outfit E.K. Brigham sold to J.B. Matthews

- 1 pair bay geldings, Tom 12 years, Sam 9 years, their total weight was 3,400 pounds
- 1 pair black and bay geldings, Nig 10 years, Barney 11 years, their total weight was 3,200 pounds
- 8 logging harnesses
- 120 camp blankets
- 4 complete sets logging sleighs
- 6 pair big drays
- 1 water tank and a sleigh with a heater
- 1 big road cutter
- 2 lumber wagons
- 2 sets big wheels (10½ feet)
- Rafting outfit including three 200-pound anchors, tie and boom chains
- 1 camp cooking range
- 1 large camp heater
- Cooking outfit for 60 men
- 1 dozen cross-cut saws
- 1 carpenter's tool outfit
- 1 complete blacksmith outfit, forge and tools
- General camp for 8 teams and 60 men
- 1 all-purpose tow chain

Ashland District Lumber Inspectors Records

55

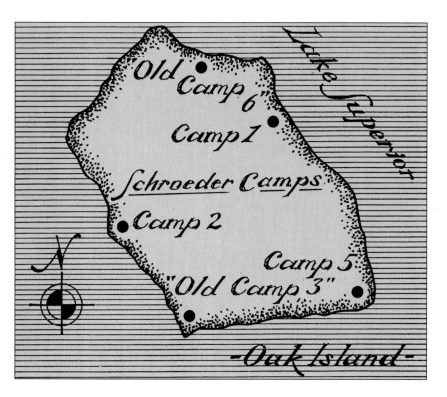

Oak Island

Oak Island is 4 miles long and 3 miles wide with about 5,000 acres. Oak Island is the highest island at an altitude of 480 feet above sea level. It has steep ravines, clay banks, sandstone cliffs, forested shore, rocky and sandy beaches.

James Chapman and William Knight of Bayfield formed a partnership to expand their Oak Island wood yard in 1870. The first year they improved the barn and several small buildings and added a 100-foot dock. By spring 1871, they'd cut approximately 2,500 cords of hemlock and hardwood.

In 1892, John Carvel cut white pine on the island. In 1893, R. D. Pike owned most of Oak Island, including the landings. He set up several camps to cut white pine. The Sandspit area was Pike's biggest camp because it had the best landing. By 1901, the harvest of white pine was nearly completed. Pike sold Schroeder his timberlands on Oak and Outer islands in 1905. An Ashland County plat book showed Schroeder owning all but a few tracts of Oak Island, including the landing sites.

Schroeder's five camps on Oak Island were linked by roads, and all had good landings. Camp No. 1 was on the northeast shore, Camp No. 2 on the west shore, Sandspit Logging Camp which was also called Camp No. 3 in the southwest corner, (there was no Camp No. 4), Camp No. 5 on the southeast shores and Camp No. 6 at the northern end.

In July 1920, 15 million board feet of logs from the previous winter's cut was towed from Oak Island to Schroeder's Ashland mill. Schroeder cut hemlock and hardwoods on Oak Island.

Camp 1

Schroeder signed a contract with C. W. Smith of Bayfield in October 1927, for all remaining timber on Oak Island. Over the winter, Schroeder logged 10 million feet of timber. Schroeder had 25 men and five horse teams on the island in 1929.

Camp 2

The R.D. Pike Lumber Company logged white pine in this area in the 1890s. From 1917 to 1929 Schroeder logged mainly hardwoods. In 1928, a vast amount of timber on Oak Island was waiting to be shipped.

A 1979 archeological survey identified 12 structural remains at this campsite, including the camp office, blacksmith shop and stable. The camp trash dump included bottles, pieces of metal, animal bones, wagon parts, even the camp safe. Today Camp No. 2 is a National Park Service campground and dock site.

Sandspit Logging Site ("Old Camp 3")

This southwest corner received some of the earliest and heaviest use of any lakeshore site. The first recorded Apostle Island logging operation began here in 1855. Schroeder started logging hemlock and hardwoods in 1919. After Schroeder abandoned Camp 3, an area resident, Martin Kane, set up housekeeping in the filers shack and used the blacksmith shop for storage. An archeological survey located building foundations, old roads and fishing remains.

Schroeder's Oak Island Camp No. 2

From Ashland on Superior Lake
a little voyage I did take.
Out to an Island was a boat
Brower, which is used to tote.

Accommodations were the best
I was a Lumber Baron's guest.
But I had to pay a six-bit fare
stowed like cargo anywhere.

I made the passage safe enough
though water was not very rough.
The course the Skipper steered was true
and soon we moored at Camp #2.

There were some passengers aboard
who went ashore when she was moored.
Some ladies who did not get sick
because they made the voyage quick.

I went ashore with my soft sack
and in the cook shack
I sat down at my place
and fed my face.

Got outside of a bunch of food
was hungry and it tasted good.
The Bull-Cook showed me where to sleep
I had to double up two deep.
A donkey's breakfast was my bed
with coat beneath my wooden head.

Next was Sunday, all day long
with nothing to do, only grow strong.
Boil up my rags, wash, mend and shave
and all my pay, or whiskey, save.

At night some things disturbed my rest
for I was in a bed bugs nest.
And they were hungry as the deuce
the bunk not having been in use.
Next morn they turned me out at five
badly chewed up, but still alive.

The Push gave me a two-bit axe
and turned me out with the Lumber Jacks.
At eleven o'clock they brought over feed
which caused a terrible stampede.
We got it catch-as-catch you can
just helped ourselves from pot to pan.

The Garbage-Go-Devil brought out
some pork and beans and sauerkraut,
bread, spuds with jackets and meat
and many other things to eat.

Those hemlock knots one as some use
they made me hungry as the deuce.
I worked from daylight to dark
chopped all knots close to the bark.

If knots are long, the Skinners kick
and horses pull until they're sick.
I slashed my way through jungle dense
hunting for logs, at the expense of

Johnny Schroeder with my axe
a weapon used by Lumber Jacks.
Alex John McKinnon was Head Squeeze
the man I had to try and please.
To do whatever he would ask
was not so difficult a task.

Camp 5

A 1981 archeological survey showed evidence of many buildings, submerged dock cribs and dump areas at this site.

Camp 6

Old Camp 6, recessed behind a sandy beach in a large bay, was protected from the northeast wind. A major ravine and a small stream bed opened out to the beach, creating a large flat area where lumberjacks staged logs. During winter, they rolled logs in the ravine and dammed the stream's mouth. In spring, meltwater filled the ravine, the dams were opened and the logs spewed into the lake to be boomed, then towed to Ashland.

R.D. Pike began logging here in 1893. Although remote, it was a main camp because of the great boat landing and log staging area. The Bayfield Press reported in 1929 that 80 men and 12 teams of horses were taken from Camp 6 to Ashland. This camp closing signaled the end of 12 years of logging on Oak Island and the cutting of over three million feet of hemlock and hardwood by the Schroeder Company.

Michigan Island

Michigan Island is 3½ miles long, 1¼ miles wide with almost 1,600 acres. This island has sandy beaches, clay cliffs and land rising 90 feet above the lake. Its east end has a sand bar about three feet deep that reaches to Gull Island. Two lighthouses in the southern end, the first built in 1857 and the second in 1869, helped guide vessels through the islands.

Schroeder logged Michigan Island from 1919 through 1923. This logging operation was very different from other camps, because in 1918 Schroeder built a logging railroad. Prior to this, the island was not logged in winter because of strong prevailing currents that prevented the formation of solid ice, making crossing between camp and the mainland unsafe. With a railroad, logging was done in the summer, although the black flies, mosquitoes, no-seeums and the heat and humidity of July and August must have presented a formidable challenge to the men.

The Second Squeeze or Straw-Boss Jack
was right there with strong mind and back.
He was on the job from morn 'til night
and treated all the fellows right.
The Third Squeeze was in full command
of the Sawyers, I understand
and had a very pleasant way
for he was born of "common clay."

The man who wielded pen and ink
thought he was an important "Gink."
Much better than us common men
because he could sling ink with pen.

The Cooks were good at making bread
the pastry was not made of lead.
The meat was tender believe me
things seasoned as they need to be.

The Flunkies were all very neat
and kept the dishes full of meat.
The coffee pot would not go dry
nothing escaped their watchful eye.

The Bull-Cooks kept the shantys clean
hauled wood and water in between.
Fed hogs and chickens, milked some cows
and had the Skinners to arouse.

The Carpenter made shavings fly
and chips ascend into the sky.
He butchered wood at such a rate
I fear he'll clean the whole darn state.

The Blacksmith made the anvil ring
shod all the horses they could bring.
He also shod the logging sleighs
earned all the wages Schroeder pays.

The Skinners hollered "Gee" and "Haw"
until, I think, it hurt their jaw.
Some horses names were so darn queer
I would not even repeat them here.

The Barn Boss fed the horses hay
and gave them oats three times a day.
Cleaned out their stalls, made their beds
but no pillows for their heads.

They had two Jammers decking logs
two Sky Hookers, and two Old River Hogs.
Who shouted "Go back for Hook-Tenders
who pull the slack, for camp Hook Men
who were tailing down,
and those two Scalers both named Brown."

There were a few Road Monkeys though
how much they monkeyed, I do not know.
I didn't monkey with them see
because they monkeyed not with me.

There was a laundry where we could
have all our duds washed very good.
A thing most men appreciate
for washing is a job they hate.

I've used enough paper and ink
describing Schroeders camp I think.
So guess I'll quit wasting my time
pen, ink, paper, writing rhyme.

Written by the Schroeder Lumber Company "sailors." Laura McKinnon
Pearson (Howard), granddaughter of Alex McKinnon, presented it to the
Ashland Historical Society.

Reprinted with permission.

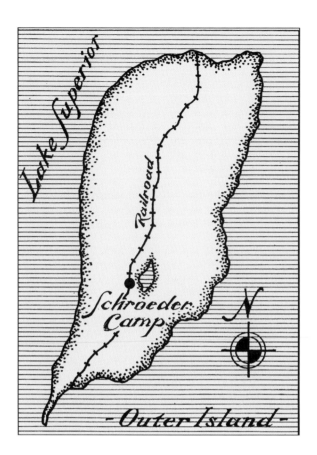

Outer Island

Outer Island is 6¼ miles long. At the northern end it is 2½ miles wide; the southern end tapers to a narrow sand point. This island, the third largest of the Apostles, contains about 8,000 acres. It has rock cliffs, cave formations and red clay banks. An inland lake about 25 feet from Lake Superior is about a quarter-mile long, 400 feet wide and about eight feet deep.

The lighthouse on the north end was built in 1874. Perched on a bluff 40 feet above the lake, the lighthouse receives the full brunt of Lake Superior's weather. Outer Island, the outermost island, is 25 miles northeast of Bayfield, Wisconsin. Hemlock and white and red pine were cut in the 1880s and 1890s. Schroeder purchased timber on Outer Island in 1917 and cut an estimated 40 million board feet of hardwoods, hemlock, cedar and pine, 1924 to 1929. In 1929, Schroeder moved their logging equipment from Oak Island to Outer Island. In 1930 a crew of 225 men cut six million feet. Operations were in full swing in 1930. It's not clear when the camp closed.

Schroeder Railroad Camp

The great significance of this camp is that it represents island railroad logging. The railroad made summer logging possible and replaced winter horse and sleigh hauling. When logging was completed on Michigan Island in 1923, the tug *Ashland* and a scow transported Schroeder's logging and railroad equipment to Outer Island.

Schroeder's Camp was next to the railroad grade in the south central area. During the summer of 1923, Schroeder crews constructed five miles of main railroad line which bisected the island in a north/south direction, plus several spurs and a dock. Spurs from the main railroad line made it possible to get logs from remote areas. In the swampy area near the beaver dam they put down a mat of full-length trees before the ties were laid. Temporary ties and rails were known as "skeleton tracks."

Locomotives were small, generally 50 to 75 tons. Schroeder had two standard gauge locomotives, a Shay (geared engine) and a Mogul (rod engine). The Shay, a short-haul engine, carried heavy loads and turned sharp, although it didn't move very fast. Generally eight to 10 cars were stacked with logs that were chained down to hold them in place. The Shay was the best known of the geared locomotives used in logging because it was extremely adaptable. Its cylinders were upright on the engineer's side, and the boiler was offset to balance the cylinders. A propeller shaft driven by cranks along one side of the engine was geared to the axles.

Courtesy The Fred Mackie Collection

Between 1874 and 1944, E. Shay in Michigan built 2,771 Shay engines.

Courtesy The Fred Mackie Collection

This Mogul engine is pulling cut logs.

Lumber camp boiled dinner

 2 whole hams
12 medium onions, cut up
 4 large rutabagas, cubed in one inch pieces
 3 large heads of cabbage, chopped
20 pounds carrots, peeled and cut in ½ inch slices
50 pounds potatoes, peeled and quartered

Salt, black and cayenne pepper, bay leaves and paprika.

In two 20-quart kettles, boil hams for four hours. Remove the hams from the kettles and save broth. Cut the meat off the bones and add it to the broth. Put 4 to 5 bay leaves in each pot. Add onion and rutabagas. Cook for approximately 30 minutes. Add carrots and cook another 30 minutes. Add cabbage and potatoes and bring to a boil. Cook until potatoes are tender. Season with whatever other spices you wish.

Serves 150-175.

This recipe is from Marcella (Lueloff) Hanninen. Her mother, Delma (Neier) Lueloff, was the cook for the Patsy Lake logging camp run by Arthur Lueloff, her husband, in the early 1930s. Marcella lived at the camp as a young child.

Walter Bender, an Ashland logging and railroad historian, ran the No. 2 engine for the Schroeder Lumber Company on Outer Island. In a letter he stated, "It was a very dangerous job. There was an unloading dock on Lake Superior, that held 10 cars. In the two miles from the camp to the unloading dock, the grade dropped 196 feet, and there were only hand brakes on the cars. The engineer who ran the engine before I did could not get along with the brakeman and had many runaways. Sometimes he would get as far as the dock before he got the train stopped. The Shay on the island was C/N #954, which came from Presque Island Lumber Company."

After the timber on the island was exhausted, the locomotives were left on the docks, and by the late '30s they were cut up for scrap, loaded on a lake vessel and sold in Duluth. Several large pieces of machinery related to steam locomotives are still at this camp.

Horse—tired of life

July 13, 1905, Ashland Daily Press

Deliberate Case of Suicide at LaPointe Walks into the Bay and Deliberately—Drowns—Was Sick

We often hear of a human being committing suicide, but for an animal to do so is rare. Yet such was certainly the case at Madeline Island Wednesday when a horse belonging to Mr. Tann deliberately walked into the waters of the bay and committed suicide by drowning. The horse had been sick for a few days and evidently concluded that if the balance of its life was to be spent in misery, the sooner it was over, the better.

A veterinarian had been called in the morning and had pronounced the horse very sick with but a small chance of recovery. Whether the horse understood the verdict of the veterinarian or not, of course, is a question that everyone must decide for himself. They say every horse has what is known as "horse sense." So the animal undoubtedly understood its condition and concluded to end its misery as soon as possible.

It walked down to the shore and began wading in the water. Several persons saw the animal walk into the water but thought nothing of it until it walked beyond its depth. Then several row boats put out and formed in a semi-circle between the animal and the open bay, trying to drive it back to the shore, but the animal plunged forward into deeper water, until it got out to the end of the dock. When one of the men in a row boat got too near, the horse threatened to turn the boat over and the man got out of the way quickly, giving the horse an opening to deep water. The boats gave chase, but the horse swam rapidly and kept ahead of them. Then one of the men on the dock started out with a gasoline launch to capture the animal. When the horse saw the launch coming, its "horse sense" told it that it could not swim faster than the launch and it deliberately poked its head under the water. By the time the launch arrived, only a few seconds or minutes at the most, the troubles of the horse were over. The launch formed a funeral party and towed the dead animal ashore, where it was given a burial. The first case of a horse committing suicide in this locality passed into history.

CHAPTER FOUR

Schroeder's
Ashland Mill

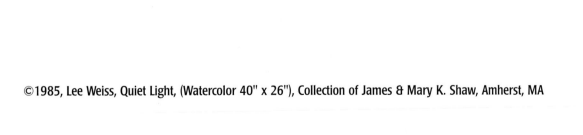

J.W. Schroeder's Lumber Company looking south.

Schroeder's sawmill and pond in Bayfield, Wisconsin.

Schroeder bought the mill in 1901

Beginning in the early 1900s, over a dozen lumber mills lined the Ashland lakefront. The John Schroeder Company bought the Pope saw and planing mill on January 10, 1901, at a bankruptcy sale. Many northern Wisconsin and Minnesota sawmills had shut down because of a lagging lumber market and the difficulty in obtaining logs. Newspapers reported an estimated 200 million board feet was held up because of drought-reduced rivers and streams.

The mill Schroeder purchased was originally built in 1884 by a Mr. Barber. In 1897 it was sold to the Pope Lumber Company. At that time its capacity for a 20-hour mill run was 160,000 board feet. The dock and yard had a capacity of 15 million feet. By 1900, this mill had produced 15,679,000 board feet of lumber.

The sawmill, appraised at $16,000, was one of Ashland's oldest properties. Schroeder also purchased the adjacent Mowatt site to expand his lumberyards and planing mill. For a total purchase price of $30,000, Schroeder owned six blocks with 1,800 feet of lakefront, good docks, fine boomage grounds, a sawmill and planing mill and a machine shop. Captain C. H. Ellis handled the transaction for Schroeder.

Immediately Schroeder upgraded the mill and added an electric light plant for $10,000. The goal was to prepare the mill for the arrival of spring logs.

Schroeder considered buying a mill in Duluth or Grand Marais, Minnesota. One of the reasons Ashland was chosen was because it was one mile closer to Duluth than was Cross River. In addition, the Apostle Islands and their sheltered waters provided protection for tugs and log rafts during bad weather. Minnesota's North Shore provided no protection for towing rafts. Tugs pulling log rafts to Ashland had to negotiate only 34 miles of open water between Cross River and the first most westerly Apostle Island, Sand Island.

John Walters, an Ashland, Wisconsin, native, worked all his life in forestry. After retirement he focused on keeping Ashland's history alive.

Employment

Ashland's 14,000 residents were thrilled with the Schroeder purchase and the prospects of employment. Area newspapers claimed Schroeder's purchase would employ an army of men for 20 years. Under the supervision of J. C. Clark, the Schroeder mill became one of the largest and best-equipped mills in the North, producing an average of 50 million board feet per year.

In 1901, the Schroeder Company ranked as a million-dollar operation that produced finished lumber, lath, ties and shingles. Its initial 24-hour run was 200,000 feet of pine and hemlock.

Lumber companies often traded log rafts when one mill was running short on logs. The Edward Hines Lumber Company contracted with Schroeder to saw eight million board feet at $2.25 per thousand feet in the spring of 1901. This enabled the mill to run continuously until logs were rafted from the Cross River. By May 1901, a night shift was added to process W. H. Gilbert's logs. In November 1901, when all the other Ashland mills shut down, only the Schroeder mill still operated. The Ashland Daily Press reported on December 4, 1902, that 202,350,000 feet of logs had landed at the Ashland docks that season.

"The Schroeder mill helped fuel Ashland's economy for over 30 years," said John Walters, an Ashland native. "It was one of the longest continuous operations of any Ashland mill. Mill work was seasonal, although the planing mill generally operated throughout the winter. Summer employment was always highest. Winter shutdowns and layoffs were common and expected. Previously employed workers were the first hired back. Work depended on the availability of logs and lumber orders." As soon as Lake Superior was navigable, logs were brought to the mill and work began. During the winter of 1904, ice fields extended 120 miles out from Ashland with an average thickness of 26 inches. In March 1905, ice fields 18 inches thick extended 10 miles from Ashland.

May 9, 1902

Ashland Mill

WANTED!

Men to Load
Cordwood on Cars
Pay $35 to 40 Per
Month with Board

Ashland Mill

**BARK PEELERS
WANTED**

50 Bark Peelers at
$2.75 Per Cord
4 Lumber Graders
at $2.50 Per Day

The winter of 1917 ice was six feet thick in Chequamegon Bay. That spring the northeasters drove this ice up on Ashland's shore.

Mill employment fluctuated between 50 and 350 men. In 1890, Ashland mill worker salaries averaged between $1.25 and $2.50 per day. Sawyers, filers and scalers had jobs similar to those in logging camps. Mill employees included a superintendent, boom master, yard master, foremen, laborers, yardmen, saw operators, graders, lumber markers, lumber checkers and shipping clerks.

The milling process

Tugs brought log rafts into the harbor where they were transferred from the rafting boom to the mill pond. Mill workers grabbed onto the logs with pike poles. Logs were fed onto a continuously moving chain called a bull chain. The logs rocked and slid back and forth on the chain as they were pulled up an incline to the mill's second floor. There the logs were transferred from the bull chain to a carriage, which took them to the saws. Men guided and pushed logs through the circular saws. Cuts were made on all four sides to square the log. The squared log was sent to the gang saw where multiple boards were cut. Different saws (band, gang and circular) were used. The goal for each log was to produce the maximum board feet of lumber. Sharp mill saws were indifferent to men who fed them. Clothing was caught, arms, fingers and lives were lost. Ashland's Rinehard Hospital witnessed the results of many workers' encounters with big, sharp saws.

Sawn lumber was picked up and sent down a series of rollers that looked like a long table. Until the 1880s, lumber was air dried, which took about a year. Kiln-dried lumber was more desirable than undried or green lumber. Schroeder's kiln drying took weeks. Once dry, it was sorted and stacked. Horses pulled lumber carriers on wooden tramways high above the ground to load the vessels that carried lumber to Schroeder's Milwaukee yards and beyond.

Workers strike

Mill workers from The Setters and Carriage Riders Unions demanded pay increases in May 1903. Setters wanted a raise of 50¢ per day—from $2.50 to $3. Carriage Riders wanted a 25¢ increase—from $2. per day to $2.25. All the other mill unions honored their strike.

Schroeder mill transfer chain employees struck for better wages in May 1916. They asked for a 25¢-per-day increase from $2.25 to $2.50. After a one-day strike, they settled for a 10¢ raise.

The Ashland Daily Press, May 28, 1903

Courtesy The John Walters Collection

Schroeder Lumber Company looking east. Note the wood waste burner in the upper right corner.

Rafting and lumber measurements

John Walters' chart compares cords, board feet, acres and city blocks.

Cords	Board Feet	City Blocks	Acres
2	1,000	---	---
1,000	500,000	1.17	6
2,000	1,000,000	2.33	12
3,000	1,500,000	3.50	18
4,000	2,000,000	4.16	24
5,000	2,500,000	5.83	30

Kindling was used in houses heated by wood stoves, heaters, fireplaces and coal-burning furnaces.

Slabwood

When logs were cut, bark slabs fell to the floor. They were piled outside and at most mills were considered waste. "From the very beginning, Schroeder found ways to minimize waste in all aspects of the company," John Walters noted. Bark and cut ends fueled furnaces that powered the mill. Schroeder used slabs to make docks and lath and later chipped it. They also sold it as kindling. Slabwood and edgings were cut into stove-size pieces and delivered in wagonloads.

Lath

Lath was a lumber by-product. Schroeder cut thinly slabbed wood with a small circular saw into strips 4 feet long, then packaged 50 strips to a bundle. It was used as the basis for solid plastered walls in buildings before wallboard. Most frame houses of the 19th century used lath over studs then covered it with plaster. In 1901, in a 10-hour run, Schroeder produced 40,000 pieces of lath.

Shingles

The first machine that produced 50,000 shingles a day was patented in 1865. Schroeder made shingles from 3-foot-long cedar logs. The shingle saw, a large, horizontal circular saw, cut the wedged shingle shape. It had a tilting movable table, which made it possible to cut each successive "slice." Rough shingles were tossed into a bin for the knot sawyers to cut and trim. The knot saw, also called a "finger-cutter," was a small, high-speed circular saw used to get the edges straight. The finished shingle was put in a bin for sorting and baling. Shingles, no two of which were exactly alike, were stacked in layers and compressed, then wrapped with metal straps into tight bundles. The Schroeder mill produced 70,000 shingles in a 10-hour run in 1901.

Hemlock

At first, only the bark from hemlock was marketable. The bark contains tannin, a chemical that cures animal hides into durable leather. Before a hemlock log was peeled, the branches were removed. Peelers used sharp knives to cut around the log's circumference. The bark was split lengthwise and peeled off in sections. The bark was laid out to dry, inner side up. Once dry, it was stacked in piles. Bark collection usually took place in late spring, when logging activities were winding down.

Starting in the 1920s, hemlock was used for lumber. As the pulpwood industry grew, peeled logs were sold to paper companies.

Railroad ties

Schroeder used decay-resistant cedar, tamarack and hemlock for railroad ties. The smaller second-growth trees were preferred, because a single tie could be made from each one. Ties were either hand-hewn or mill-sawed. Hand-hewn cedar logs were scored with a double-bitted axe. Cuts were made on each side of the log, then a broad axe with its chisel-shaped cutting edge was used to make sweeping strokes in the opposite direction from which the scoring cuts were made. This smoothed each side of the log, which now measured seven-by-nine inches. A cross-cut saw cut the hewn log into the required nine-foot lengths. Hand-hewn ties were considered superior because they had a smoother surface which made them last longer. Each mile of railroad track used 2,700 ties.

A quick rescue

In June 1925, an 18-year-old Schroeder mill employee was driving a horse pulling four loads of lumber. The chain between the horse and the first load ran over a board and it changed the direction of the loads. The boy saw what was going to happen and reached for the pin to release the horse from the chain attached to the loads, but it was too late and the horse was dragged after the lumber. In the horse's struggle to keep from going over the edge of the tram, it knocked the boy down and fell directly upon him. Just as the horse was slipping over the edge of the tram, mill employees rushed and rescued the boy and horse. The boy suffered a crushed knee cap.

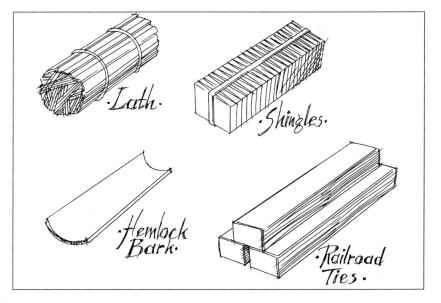

Years ago

In the old days, before water or steam power, lumber was cut by two men, one standing above the log on a platform and the second standing in a pit below the log. Together they pushed and pulled the saw back and forth. By the time logging reached Lake Superior, power circular saws were used.

Bringing a raft into Ashland.

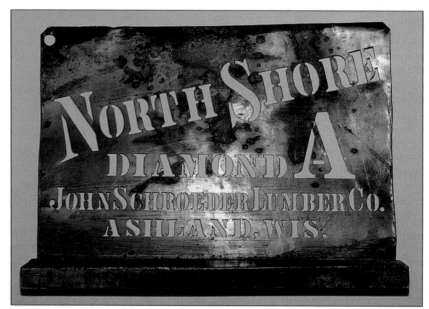

John Schroeder lumber stencil.

Stacked lumber was loaded on Schroeder vessels at the dock.

Distance from Ashland by water

Washburn, WI – 6 miles

Bayfield, WI – 17 miles

Two Harbors, MN – 71 miles

Duluth, MN – 93 miles

Isle Royale, MI – 115 miles

Port Arthur, Ontario, Canada – 164 miles

Ontonagon, MI – 74 miles

Sault Sainte Marie, MI – 348 miles

Cross River, MN – 70 miles

Grand Marais, MN – 80 miles

Sugarloaf Cove, MN – 62 miles

Lumber piled at the Schroeder yard.

Boom years

In mid-April 1902, as soon as the ice went out, the log rafting season began with the arrival of 50 million feet of North Shore logs. The mill started humming and ran day and night through October. Over 200 million feet of logs was rafted to Ashland that year. Ashland's port receipts were reported at $2.4 million, with an average price of $12 per thousand feet.

Slow lumber sales in 1903 created an abundance of lumber at Schroeder's docks in 1904. In April 1905, the mill started cutting North Shore logs, employing both day and night shifts. By fall, the mill had exceeded a 25 million feet output in seven months. In a 20-hour run, mill workers cut 200,000 feet of pine and hemlock lumber. From May to August, Schroeder employed 150 mill workers, plus 300 men who cut and transported logs and 100 men who peeled hemlock bark. The mill opened with a day shift in early May 1906, to saw Apostle Island logs. The night shift began in mid-June. Mill manager Mr. V. Young reported that 1906 was a banner season. In May 1908, the mill began with only a day shift.

Schroeder fire

Logs from the North Shore and Apostle Islands kept the lumber mill operating until fire destroyed Schroeder's lumber yards on August 21, 1909. The company lost 15 million board feet. The fire was started by a spark from a burner and aggravated by high winds. Employees caught on the tramway were forced to jump into the lake to save their lives. Fire fighters used dynamite to disperse the fire and save the Central Ore dock and planing mill.

In April 1910, the rebuilt mill started cutting. It shut down the first week of September for a period of two weeks because a drought held up 12 million feet of logs near Saxon, Wisconsin.

Pulpwood

"The paper industry was transformed when wood pulp replaced using rags and straw," according to John Walters. In 1879, wood pulp was 3.5 percent of the raw material used to make paper. By 1899, that figure had jumped to 52 percent. Various trees produced paper of different types and quality. Selection depended on the length of the fibers, and the gums and resins contained in the wood. Initially, eight-foot logs with a 16-inch base and eight-inch diameter were required. This meant the majority of tree parts was left in the woods. Later, this size specification was reduced to seven inches, then to six. Trees supplied the raw material for the nation's wallpaper and publishing industries.

Pulpwood rafts replaced log rafts. Ashland's first pulpwood raft came from Minnesota's North Shore in 1910. Pulpwood rafts were not towed into Superior and Duluth harbors because they were too big to pass through the narrow channels. By comparison, Ashland's large harbor provided an easy approach.

Schroeder had one of Ashland's first pulpwood hoists. Logs were hoisted from the mill pond, hand-loaded onto rail cars and shipped downstate to the Wisconsin River Valley mills. A double shift loaded 24 cars each day. Loading pulpwood employed, on the average, 50 men each year. In 1921, a day and night shift, each working 10 hours, loaded 40 cars with spruce pulpwood. Every 48 hours the loading process was repeated. Schroeder's reign ended in 1923, when Consolidated Paper Company got into rafting and constructed its own pulpwood loading hoist.

Courtesy The John Walters Collection

Pulpwood hoist on tramway facing Schroeder's mill pond and stacked lumber.

John Schroeder Lumber Mill, Ashland, Wisconsin.

The impact of war

In 1914, Schroeder hoped the European War would have little effect on the demand for lumber, thinking that farmers had good crops and would continue to buy lumber. Although there was fear the lumber market would decline, the day shift continued. The mill cut 10 million feet, employing 100 men who cut 100,000 feet. However, most of this lumber remained stacked on the docks. Ashland mill manager Frank Clark reduced his crew by half. In September 1914, more than 100 night-shift employees were dismissed because of depressed conditions throughout the country. The European crisis had caused a gradual tightening of money. This business slump was attributed to over-production, export trade reduction and the war. Only three Schroeder winter logging camps continued to operate.

In 1915, 30 men loaded pulpwood all summer. The last pulpwood raft containing 8,000 cords, worth $50,000, arrived from Port Arthur, Ontario, Canada, on September 9. The Schroeder mill operated all season until navigation closed.

Business began looking up

The mill reopened in May 1916, employing 300 men. Manager Frank Clark was quoted in the Ashland Daily Press: "The old familiar whistle is sweet music to the ears of these men." A double shift worked throughout the season. At the height of the pulpwood season, Schroeder's monthly payroll reached $20,000. In May 1916, an 800,000-foot hemlock raft and a hardwood scow arrived from the island camps. In June, Schroeder contracted to drive piles and extend the ferry boat landing for the Ashland Commercial Docks. In June, a scow brought 500 cords of pulpwood from Grand Marais, Minnesota. In July, a 6,000-cord pulpwood raft arrived from Canada. The first

600,000-foot spruce and pine log raft in two years came from the Cross River. In August, the third 4,000-cord pulpwood raft arrived from Canada.

By 1917, the war had created a demand for pulpwood, and business began looking up. Ashland was the only Great Lakes port receiving pulpwood rafts from Canada. In April 60,000 cords of pulpwood were rafted from Nipigon Bay, Ontario, Canada. In September, the eighth and last raft of the season bearing 7,000 cords of pulpwood arrived from Port Arthur, Canada.

Two tugs towed a 5,000-cord pulpwood raft valued at $40,000 from Port Arthur, Canada, in July 1918. Weeks later, 90 million feet came from Bessemer, Michigan. It was speculated that Bessemer would produce enough hemlock and hardwoods to keep the mill running for years.

In 1919, the Schroeder mill sawed 1.5 million logs from Ontonagon, Michigan, for the Lakeshore Lumber Company. A night shift helped process the 10 million feet of logs in the mill pond. The tugs *Ashland, Henry F. Brower* and *Saugatuck* hauled four pulpwood rafts to Ashland. The *J. C. Ames, Erna, Traveler* and *Ashland* brought pulpwood rafts from Nipigon Bay, Canada. In addition, more Apostle Island logs were ready to raft. In September, Schroeder purchased 90 million feet of hemlock and hardwoods from Bessemer, Michigan. Schroeder shipped over four million feet of hemlock that year.

In 1920, the first raft arrived on July 15. In June 1921, Frank Clark reported, "They now had enough logs to keep the mill crew busy all summer." On July 9 another raft arrived. A second 15-million-foot log raft was expected from Oak Island. Two tugs brought a 6,000-cord pulpwood raft valued at $60,000 from Port Arthur, Canada. This raft took 10 days to load. The *J.C. Ames* brought two North Shore pulpwood rafts.

Lost logs meant lost jobs

"Schroeder Mill Closes Down—A $75,000 Hemlock Log Raft Was Lost." The raft's boom sticks broke during a fierce storm near Outer Island in the Apostles. Mill workers had been waiting for this log raft. Immediately, 300 mill employees were laid off for the season.

The Ashland Daily Press

Manufacturing hemlock chips

By June 1921, mill work was divided between processing logs into lumber and loading pulpwood. Schroeder, aware of Consolidated's decisions, decided to modernize its equipment to chip hemlock slabs, instead of selling hemlock slabs for firewood.

Chipped hemlock was in demand from the paper industry because it saved money hauling and cutting logs. Chipping was the most economical method of bringing spruce, balsam, fir, jack pine and aspen to Wisconsin paper mills. Schroeder's chip-making machinery was manufactured in Milwaukee. To house its new equipment, Schroeder constructed a 30-by-100 foot building and a 14-by-100 foot chip storage bin. By July 1922, the chipping mill employed 15 people.

The beginning of the end

The mill closed unexpectedly in October 1925, putting 300 men out of work after a $75,000 raft was torn apart in a fierce wind and lost. It was anticipated the mill would close in November. Frank Brown announced the mill would reopen in May 1926, with 200 employees. In September of that year, the mill closed and laid off 150 men along with another 200 at Outer Island camp. The mill opened again with 260 men in May 1927. They expected steady work when Oak Island rafts arrived. The planing mill had been operating continuously since January with 88 men. Once the lake ice went out in April 1929, the mill opened, employing 175 men. With only about three weeks of work, they were waiting for the Oak Island rafts with enough logs for about two months. Brown opened the planing mill in March 1930, with 40 men.

The end

The Schroeder Company held on for another decade, but finally on July 11, 1939, Ashland County acquired the tax deed to the Schroeder mill and its personal property. The Schroeder Company denied the validity of the tax deed and took the issue to Circuit Court. On Nov 16, 1939, the Ashland County Board offered to sell (cash only) its right, title and interest on the Schroeder property for $14,000 or the property, without the land, for $8,000. On December 13, the Schroeder Company purchased the personal property, including buildings, improvements, machinery, tools and property for $8,000. Ashland County kept the land. On December 16, Schroeder's controller and spokesman Harold Smith indicated the company planned to operate the mill and employ at least 40 men for at least three months. They agreed to dismantle the buildings if the mill did not resume operations. They sold all surplus machinery and kept enough to operate on a smaller scale. At this time, Fred Schroeder, John's son, was president of the company. In 1939, the company sold its Milwaukee yards and disposed of all their property.

Mind-boggling statistics

The 1940 publication "Lumber Industry and Its Workers" claimed, "If all the white pine cut between 1776 and 1940 in this country was piled on a city block, the pile would reach about 400 miles high, roughly 75 mountains the height of Mt. Everest."

This 2,400,000,000,000,000 (two quadrillion, four hundred trillion) board feet built

- 52 million homes,
- 12 million farm houses,
- 2 million schools and libraries,
- 650,000 churches and
- 450,000 factories.

Aerial view of the John Schroeder Lumber Company

CHAPTER FIVE

Conclusion

The American dream

The story of John Schroeder was the realization of the American dream. John worked hard and earned a reputation for honesty and integrity. He died on October 22, 1908, a successful man. His success was no small accomplishment.

Little remains from a century ago. Margaretha died in 1913 at age 72. Their home was sold in 1918 and it became St. Joseph's Home for the Aged. In 1950, the home was turned into a 68-room hotel. Soon after it was demolished. Schroeder's Milwaukee mansion is gone. The ground where the mansion once stood is now dead-center within a housing project. Schroeder's lumber yards, docks and offices are gone. St. John's Evangelical Lutheran Church, now Milwaukee's fourth-oldest church, still stands, but has only a handful of members.

Schroeder, the town

The town of Schroeder, Minnesota, was once called Cross River, then Redmyer and before that Tchibaiatigo-zibi in Ojibwa, which means "Spirit of wood of the Soul River." Schroeder, the town, was named after a person who, in the custom and wisdom of his time, came, took and left. John's death came only three years after the Cross River operation closed. His three sons, John Jr., Fred and William, kept the business going another three decades.

Looking back, some people feel the logging company damaged the area beyond any justification. Some claim the Cross River doesn't hold as much water as it did years ago when the trees were there to hold it. The dams held back large amounts of water during the time Schroeder logged. Now the water drains so quickly there's little water in summer.

A man of sterling honesty

At John Schroeder's memorial service, he was characterized as a family man, a man of sterling honesty, a Christian gentleman, charitable and kind to those in need and an exemplary citizen of his adopted country. John served as vice-president of The Concordia Fire Insurance Company, which focused its business within Milwaukee's Lutheran community. John was a second district alderman for eight years. For 11 years he was a member of the Old Volunteer Fire Department on Engine Neptune No. 2. He belonged to The Old Settlers Club and The Milwaukee Sharpshooter's Club. As a democrat of the old school, he believed in democracy as a form of true republicanism and was known to support competent, honest Republicans in preference to Democrats.

Old Settlers Memorial Book

The top soil on the North Shore produced good crops for a short time—then gave out.

The trees

Today, one can only imagine the unspoiled natural beauty of the majestic white pine stands, with trees taller than a 10-story building and stumps large enough for a couple to square dance on. The forest was a mix of sugar and rock maple, yellow birch, basswood, white pine, spruce and balsam. Moose ate the balsam and left the pine alone. After the pine was gone, the shade-tolerant hardwoods were cut. Today, deer eat the white pine and leave the balsam alone.

Dynamite!

Evidence of dynamiting the Cross River is still visible from the bridge. Huge, cracked boulders eroded and tumbled down, filling and choking the bay and harbor. Logs plunging down the river and spring floods from up-country brought mud, debris and countless tons of gravel to the lower reaches of the river, forming a new sand bar at the river's mouth. Although at the turn of the century dynamiting river channels was considered common practice, today it would stimulate considerable debate.

What passed for logic was an unfounded belief that after loggers cleared the land—any land—farmers would come. Cattle could graze. Gardens could grow. Homes, churches and schools would be built, families raised, communities established. The wilderness would be tamed. The problem with this logic was that white pine grew in sandy, well-drained soil at the Cross River. This rich top soil was thin, and although the first few years crops grew quite well, the soil soon gave out.

It is difficult to identify any lasting benefits attributable to the logging done by the Schroeder Company—except, perhaps, those of the march of progress. The white pine Schroeder cut is credited with use in helping to construct the World's Fair buildings in St. Louis—the place where he spent his first years in America.

Times change

Logging dominated the community for about a decade. Then, instead of farming, fishing became the Norwegian settlers' main occupation. In the 1920s, tourists started frequenting the cool and healthy North Shore. In the 1940s, pulpwood supported the economy. In the 1950s, taconite fueled the economy, and in the 1980s, steel. By the 1990s, tourists once again became a viable source of revenue.

Consolidated Paper Company stopped rafting at Sugarloaf Cove in 1971 and in 1985 donated that land to the Nature Conservancy. The State of Minnesota purchased the site in 1988. In 1992, a portion of it, the Point, was designated as a State Scientific and Natural Area in conjunction with the Minnesota Department of Natural Resources. The Sugarloaf Interpretive Center Association (SICA) was formed to protect the natural and cultural resources, and to establish and maintain a public interpretive forum at the cove. SICA established a visitor trail in 1996. Only Consolidated's old office remains on the site.

Today, the township of Schroeder is almost entirely part of the Superior National Forest and the Finland State Forest. Trails along the river, once used by men driving logs down the river, are now used by trout fishermen and women. One Schroeder logging camp structure still stands near the mouth of the Cross River on land owned by the Lamb family. And the white pines are gone.

Courtesy The Mary Bell Collection

This building is the only remaining Schroeder structure at Cross River.

Courtesy The Mary Bell Collection

Mary Bell stands next to the new granite cross at the mouth of the Cross River where Father Baraga's wooden original once stood.

Vessels

Little other than pictures is left of any Schroeder vessels. The tug *Ashland's* whistle is on display at the Army Corps of Engineers' Museum in Duluth, Minnesota, and its propeller is at the Historical Center on Madeline Island. Ed Erickson said he was absolutely sure this was the *Ashland's* propeller, because he remembered when one of its blades was damaged and a 12-inch by 6-inch splice was used to repair it. The scows *Bob Cook* and the *Finn McCool* are submerged in Bayfield harbor. Pat Labadie has dived to see both scows and reported, "They're too fragile to bring up in anything but small pieces." The tug *Butterfield* remains on the job in East Muskegon, Michigan.

Apostle Islands

During the summer of 1930, a National Park Service representative visited Outer Island to determine whether the Apostle Islands would qualify to become a National Park. The scale and intensity of the logging that had been done at Schroeder's Outer Island railroad camp, along with the impact of other lumber companies and independent contractors, was a determining factor in the Department of Interior's rejection of the Apostle Islands as a National Park.

Time changes attitudes

In 1970, 20 of the 22 Apostle Islands and a portion of the Bayfield peninsula became the Apostle Islands National Lakeshore. At this time, logging within park boundaries terminated. This included 42,000 acres spread out over 600 square miles. In 1989, Schroeder's Trout Point Logging Camp on Stockton Island was added to the National and Wisconsin Register of Historic Places.

Schroeder's impact

Schroeder's logging had a dramatic impact on the Apostle Islands. Of the eleven historic Apostle Island logging sites, Schroeder operated seven of them. Current dock sites, campgrounds and trailheads are close to old logging sites. Only a few places along the islands' shores allow human access, therefore a campsite today was a campsite 100 years ago. Some remains of logging buildings are still visible.

At Trout Point, an unofficial archeological dig located a timber-lined watering trough near a stable, a long-handled water pump, dump areas and several large pieces of equipment, including steam locomotive parts. In 1983, a trail was constructed following the Schroeder railroad grade through the camp connecting the north Outer Island Light Station with the sandspit in the south.

Ashland

Ashland's population reached its height—14,000 residents—in 1901 because of the lumber industry. In 1901 smoke, noise, commotion, and even factory waste, were looked upon as evidence of promise and progress. Today, Ashland's population is about 8,700. No lumber mills remain.

In an Ashland park, three log raft boom sticks, a tug propeller and a big wheel remind us of a time past. "I've been staining these Sitka Spruce boom logs for 25 years, trying to keep them looking okay," John Walters lamented. "I'm afraid the fly ants are getting ahead of me." Black sawdust and slab wood still wash up along the shore. John Walters and some of the old timers get together to keep alive a past only a few remember.

Trees outfitted lives

Pine—malleable and light—was considered the most versatile building material. It was the first choice for building mansions, tenement houses and farm buildings. Once built, these structures were filled with wooden beds, tables, chairs, boxes, barrels and much more. Wood-handled tools were used to plant and harvest wheat, barley, corn, oats and rye to feed an exploding population. Wooden ships, wagons and railroad ties were necessary to transport these goods. Wood products became matches, sidewalks, even coffins.

Rafting tug propeller in Ashland's park.

Diver bringing up a sunken log from Superior's depths.

Gifts from the forests

The latest boom to the Ashland economy is, once again, a gift of trees. White pine, oak, birch, maple and hemlock logs are being pulled from Lake Superior. Those involved in this endeavor estimate that 10 to 20 percent of the logs cut around the turn of the century became waterlogged by the weight of other logs and sank. Lake Superior's icy water and low oxygen content kept the logs in cold storage, which preserved them. According to a March 5, 1992, Milwaukee Sentinel article, "Enough of this sunken wood exists to keep one sawmill buzzing 10 to 30 years."

To retrieve logs today, scuba divers attach air bags to the logs and float them to the surface where they are chained and lifted by crane onto an anchored barge. This wood is commercially valuable if sawn while still wet, then dried. If the logs are not sawn within the first 30 days, exposure to air and warmth causes them to turn to mush. These trees, cut a century ago, are extremely valuable. They are sold to make fine furniture and musical instruments.

Hardwoods grew under a canopy of pines that forced them to grow tall and straight, stretching for sunlight. Because they grew tall quickly and widened slowly, the grain of their wood is so fine that they have as many as 50 growth rings per inch. Today's wood has only six to eight growth rings per inch.

As time passes

As time passes, more conclusions will be drawn about the impact of this historic period. During the time this book was being written, a law firm expressed interest in using it as a document of record as part of a Federal grant application directed toward cleaning up Ashland's water, land and air.

As time passes the question arises about how well current land users and uses will be judged in 100 years—will contemporary standards of stewardship and global responsibility stand up to the test of time?

Courtesy The Bob Silver Collection

A 130-year-old yellow birch tree growing over a 300-year-old white pine left lying on the ground. Bob Silver cut the birch in 1955.

Bibliography

Blair, Walter A. *A Raft Pilot's Log: A History of the Great Rafting Industry on the Upper Mississippi 1840-1915*. 1930.

Burnham, Guy M. *The Lake Superior Country in History and in Story*. Paradigm Press, 1929.

Burridge, George Nau. *Green Bay Workhorses: The Nau Tug Line*. Manitowoc, Wisconsin, Maritime Museum, 1991.

Conard, Howard Louis. *History of Milwaukee, Volume II*. Milwaukee Historical Society, 1895.

Culkin, William E. *North Shore Place Names*. Wisconsin State Historical Society, Madison. Scott-Mitchell Publishing Co. St. Paul, Minnesota, 1931.

Culver, Edith Dodd. *610 Ellis and the Hospital Children*. Browzer Books, Ashland, Wisconsin, 1978.

Harris, Walt. *The Chequamegon Country 1659-1976*. Fayetteville, Arkansas, 1978.

Hughson, John and Courtney Bond. *Hurling Down The Pine*. The Historical Society of the Gatineau, 1964.

Industrial Workers of the World. *The Lumber Industry and Its Workers*. Chicago, Illinois, 1920.

John Schroeder Lumber Company. *Milwaukee Lumber Dealers Association*. Milwaukee Historical Society, 1896.

King, Frank A. *Minnesota Logging Railroads*. Golden West Books, 1923.

Lidfors, Kate. *Historic Logging Sites in the Apostle Islands National Lakeshore: A Resource Management Plan*. Apostle Islands National Lakeshore, 1984.

Longyear, J. M. *Landlooker in the Upper Peninsula of Michigan*. Marquette County Historical Society, St. Paul, Minnesota, 1960.

Milwaukee History. The Magazine of the Milwaukee County Historical Society, Autumn 1987, Vol. 10, #3.

Nelligan, John Emmett. *A White Pine Empire: The Life of a Lumberman*. North Star Press, 1929.

Old Settlers Memorial Book. Old Settlers Club, Vol. 1, October 22, 1908, Milwaukee, Wisconsin.

Pierre, Joseph H. *When Timber Stood Tall*. Superior Publishing Company, 1979.

Raff, Willis H. *Pioneers in the Wilderness*. Cook County Historical Society, Grand Marias, Minnesota, 1981.

Ryan, J. C. *Early Loggers in Minnesota*. The Minnesota Timber Producer's Association, Duluth, 1976.

Sorden, L. G. *Lumberjack Lingo*. Wisconsin House, Spring Green, Wisconsin, 1969.

Waters, Thomas F. *The Superior North Shore*. University of Minnesota Press, Minneapolis, Minnesota, 1987.

Watrous, Lieutenant Colonel Jerome A. *Memoirs of Milwaukee County, Volume II*. Milwaukee Historical Society.

Wells, Robert W. *Daylight in the Swamp*. North Word Press, 1978.

Photo captions

Sidebar Titles

Mary Bell has authored three books: *Dehydration Made Simple* (1980 Magic Mill), *Mary Bell's Complete Dehydrator Cookbook* (1994 Morrow), and *Just Jerky* (1996 The Dry Store). In addition she's written numerous articles and writes a monthly column for the *Fillmore County Journal.* She's a graduate of the University of Wisconsin and holds a master's degree from Saint Mary's College.

For more than a decade, Mary Bell and her husband, Joe Deden, have been involved in developing Eagle Bluff, a residential environmental learning center in southeastern Minnesota. The center's core mission is promoting stewardship of and responsibility for the natural world, with a special emphasis on trees.

To understand what the world of logging, rafting and milling was like a hundred years ago, Mary Bell gathered nuggets of history from a variety of sources. The men featured in *Cutting Across Time* give substance and character to this subject. Bob Silver knows the Cross River and its history. Pat Labadie, Director of the Duluth Army Corps of Engineers, knows Lake Superior vessels. In his youth, Fred Mackie worked summers on a tug hauling log rafts to Ashland. John Walters worked 40 years in Ashland mills. Ed Erickson, a native of Bayfield, Wisconsin, spent his life exploring the Apostle Islands.

Lee Weiss is an internationally acclaimed watercolorist. She has paintings in 26 public collections including the Smithsonian's National Museum of American Art, The National Air and Space Museum, The Phillips Collection and The National Museum of Women in the Arts. In 1991 she was named a Dolphin Fellow, the American Watercolor Society's highest level of recognition. Since 1970 she has been listed in *Who's Who in American Art.*

While visiting Lake Superior in 1963, Weiss stood on a long pier and looked down through 40 feet of clear, blue water. She was artistically inspired by stones in the lake bed that appeared to come to life in the play of refracted light. Her fascination with underwater stones has remained the most prominent theme of her artistic career. Weiss lives in Madison, Wisconsin.

Dale Mann's lifelong career as a commercial illustrator began at age two, when he got his first box of crayons. Out of his Evansville, Wisconsin studio he's illustrated numerous books, a variety of posters and drawings to compliment magazine and newspaper articles. Some of his biggest projects have included advertising and packaging campaigns and comprehensive business texts and manuals for large corporations. Dale's approach to each new project is to first develop a clear mental image, after that the drawing begins. Dale studied art at the University of Wisconsin in Madison.